AF493365

UNEMPLOYABLE!

THE PSYCHOLOGICAL TOLL OF PROVING YOUR WORTH

LESLIE BARBER

Unemployable!
The Psychological Tool of Proving Your Worth

Cover Design:
MAD Book Covers

ISBN:
979-8-9948108-0-4   Paperback
979-8-9948108-1-1   Kindle

For more information visit: https://www.elsiepress.com/

SETTING THE STAGE

BREADTH VS DEPTH

THE IN-BETWEEN

NETWORKING

INTERVIEWS

YOU'RE UNDERDRESSED!

WHY NOT ME?

EPILOGUE

POSTSCRIPT

Section One
Setting the Stage

Chapter 1:
Unemployable!

All I ever wanted was to change the world by doing good work. It didn't quite go as planned.

Job hunting sucks. I don't think anyone is thrilled to be on the hunt for somewhere to hang their hat. Nobody wakes up Monday morning—unemployed, broke, discouraged—and feels motivated to scroll through LinkedIn, Indeed, Monster, Ziprecruiter, or any of the other job search websites. It's a drudge. I get that and will continue to emphasize it throughout this book. Because the more I say it, the better you will feel about your own experiences.

Granted, there are some exceptions to the stress of job hunting.

Nepotism, for example. Sometimes Daddy can get you a job at the company, and you can take over when he retires. That's okay, I'm not mad about it. I just wish I had a Daddy like that.

I'm guessing farmers probably don't spend a lot of time job hunting. You get up and feed the cows and shovel poop and grow the food and get on with it, as do the kids and the grandkids. At least they did in the olden days. Factory farming is not my expertise, so for my purposes here, let's assume you live on your family farm where many generations have kept the land. You probably don't have a resume in ten different formats sitting in your hard drive. (Thank you for taking the time to read my book, though!) Otherwise, we all do it.

There are some who are recruited, going from a job to a higher-stress job to a higher-paying job. Everyone had to start somewhere. Well, most everyone. I started writing this book in 1998. Since then, I've gone through countless career transitions, requiring an ongoing reinvention of myself, my goals, and my resume. It's no fun! Luckily, I saved my rejection letters and took notes so that all these experiences can be as fresh and painful for me as they are validating and encouraging for you!

A note to any younger readers, and a painful reminder to older readers: back in the day, when I first started looking for a serious job, there was no AI. Mainly because there was no internet, and in fact, we rarely had access to a computer. We typed our resumes, using white-out to correct errors. Back then, we bought a box of fancy linen paper to type our resume and cover letter on. Once computers became more accessible, it took a few years and many terribly formatted resumes to get efficient at job hunting. Fortunately, I didn't have 40 years of job experience to try to fit onto one page back then.

Speaking of job titles accrued over four decades, here are a few of mine:

Babysitter, Gardener, Nanny, Personal Care Attendant, Usher, Science Interpreter, House Painter, Group Home Staff, Social Worker, Organic Farmer, Office Administrator, Food and Beverage Delivery Driver, Standardized Patient, Consultant, Race Director, Volunteer Coordinator, Bartender, Waitress, Sales Clerk, Baker, Patient Care Coordinator,

Operations Director, Coach, Cooking and Baking Instructor, Small Business Owner and Grant Writer.

Add in my volunteer titles, and you will see why I feel a bit disjointed when trying to explain what it is I actually *do*. Race Director, Triathlon Team Coach, Basketball Coach, HOA President, VP of Fundraising, Grant Reviewer, Theatre Booster President, Usher, and Bread Baker, not to mention Board Member and always a Committee Member of some sort. On top of all of this, I was a stay-at-home mom. Don't do the math on how I managed to do all that and stay home with the kids. There was some overlap.

I'm a master of reinvention. As you can see, I have dallied in many fields. I think that's because the perfect job hasn't come along yet. Sure, I'm almost at retirement age, but I still hold out hope that there will be a place for me, one where I work for a great organization bettering the world, where I'm well-paid and have flexible hours in which to keep a work-life balance, that gives me both health care and 401K benefits. I'd prefer to work about five hours a month for a six-figure salary. It's okay to dream!

Now that you know a little about my past, let's explore the challenge my non-traditional career path can pose to recruiters when they try to find a place for me.

BEFORE YOU TURN THE PAGE
Check every box that applies to you

- ☐ Are you good at many things?

- ☐ Are you a quick learner?

- ☐ Are you always on the lookout for a new opportunity?

- ☐ Are you disappointed in the status quo?

- ☐ Are you an outside-of-the-box thinker?

- ☐ Have you had a job?

- ☐ Have you applied for a job?

- ☐ Have you been rejected for a job?

Then

This Book Is For You.

You are not alone in this

Chapter 2:
Get A Job!

As a fast learner and highly capable human, I've always known that I have the ability to wear many hats in a work environment. I'm always looking for the opportunity to share that in a job interview setting, since my time and experience are equally valid to those of someone who's followed a more traditional career trajectory. From a very young age, I envisioned changing the world through my work, and expected that it would be obvious to anyone who met me that I'm the perfect person for any position they have on offer.

My first jobs were for survival, working to pay my way through college. After completing my undergraduate degree, I yearned for more, and quickly figured out that it was *who I knew* that could get my foot in the door. I started doing community-based social work and moved up a bit through the ranks, successfully getting hired just out of college and moving to higher pay and more demanding positions. Until my employer pulled the rug out from under me. After that, my focus shifted. I attended graduate school while working full-time at another university, hoping a Master's Degree would open doors.

I was wrong. Doors were slammed a lot more than they were opened.

'Unemployable!' explores my crazy job hunting adventures from busy college student to post-graduate school, where I took a job for which I was vastly overqualified just to be able to pay my bills. Spoiler alert: it ended badly.

Next came the interruption of motherhood and the many years trying to keep one foot in the working world and failing terribly. Finally, the painful transition into a new era of job hunting using technology.

This book will take a look at focused job searching, having come through the wringer in my life, starting as "too young" and finding that suddenly I'm "too old." In the blink of an eye, my appearance, graduation dates, and many years of experience are seen as a negative. I hope that somewhere in this book, you can relate to the challenges as well as the triumphs, finding a reason to smile along the way.

In the primary stages of job hunting, I'm an expert at jumping ahead, creating best-case outcomes for each and every job that I apply for. The further I get in the interview process, the more detailed these fantasies become. The scenarios I imagine are often very detailed. The outcomes? Well, in my fantasy, they start out as perfection. In reality, they don't always pan out. Sort of like online dating.

ONLINE DATING VS JOB HUNTING

The Dating World	The Job Hunt

THE FIRST SWIPE

You get the app and swipe whichever direction it is to say, I like you.

THE FIRST SEARCH

You see a post on a job-hunting site with a title that catches your interest, and you click on it.

THE MATCH

You match with the person you swiped on.

THE MATCH

You match the qualifications for the job and send your resume.

THE DEEP DIVE

Once you find out their name, you start doing a deep dive on their background.

THE DEEP DIVE

You research the company, finding out every last detail about it and everyone who works there.

THE FIRST INTERACTION

You reach out and say hi, and they reply.

THE FIRST INTERACTION

You get a notification that your resume has been forwarded to the hiring manager.

EARLY EXCITEMENT

Texts are exchanged. You're excited because it seems like such a perfect fit.

EARLY EXCITEMENT

You're invited to set up a phone interview. You're excited because it seems like such a perfect fit.

THE PHONE CALL

The initial phone call goes well. Casual discussion and cheerful banter end in a plan to meet in person

THE PHONE INTERVIEW

The phone interview goes well. Casual discussion and cheerful banter end in the promise of an in-person interview.

ONLINE DATING VS JOB HUNTING

The Dating World	*The Job Hunt*
PREP FOR THE COFFEE DATE You look up the menu and make sure there's good parking.	**PREP FOR THE INTERVIEW** You schedule your interview and research the office building to see what parking is like.
THE OUTFIT DILEMMA You buy a new outfit but end up wearing something from your closet. Later, you regret it.	**THE OUTFIT DILEMMA** You buy a new outfit but end up wearing something from your closet. Later, you regret it.
THE ARRIVAL You arrive early and hide in the bathroom for 20 minutes.	**THE ARRIVAL** You arrive early and sit in the parking lot for 20 minutes.
THE COFFEE SHOP ENCOUNTER Your date arrives, looking just like their photos, and you bond over common interests.	**THE INTERVIEW CONNECTION** You connect well with the interview panel, making eye contact and discovering commonalities.
THE WAITING GAME You walk away feeling like the date was a success, hoping for an encore. You wait for them to make the next move.	**THE WAITING GAME** You discuss next steps. Then, radio silence.
ANXIETY SETS IN For the next one to two weeks, you avoid texting or calling him to ask about the delay. You fantasize about your future together.	**ANXIETY SETS IN** You avoid calling or emailing the recruiter. You fantasize about your success on the job and your rapid rise through the organization.

ONLINE DATING VS JOB HUNTING

The Dating World	*The Job Hunt*

OVERTHINKING EVERYTHING

You wonder if he's been in an accident or if you made a mistake thinking there was a connection. You replay the date in your mind.

OVERTHINKING EVERYTHING

You wonder if you made a mistake in your perception of the interview or perhaps left out your contact information.

THE TEXT

Finally, you text him after days of silence. You subtly ask how he enjoyed the date.

THE FOLLOW-UP EMAIL

You finally reach out to HR, wondering what's taking them so long to get back to you.

THE AWKWARD SILENCE

One of two things happens:
1) He doesn't respond. 2) You find out he's still using the dating app.

THE AWKWARD SILENCE

One of two things happens:
1) They don't reply. 2) The job is still posted and your application status is position has been filled.

THE SOCIAL MEDIA STALK

You stalk his Instagram, seeing him with someone younger, thinner, and better educated.

THE LINKEDIN STALK

You stalk the company on LinkedIn, discovering someone younger, thinner, and better educated was hired.

THE END

THE END

You consider moving on, trying new things. Maybe that guy at the dive bar on Thursdays?

You consider selling foot photos online.

Chapter 3:
It's About The Journey

When I was in second grade, in the early 1970s, we had our IQs tested. Mine was high enough to be asked to attend a special school once a week at the newly anointed Gifted and Talented Center. The year and a half I spent there made me believe in my capabilities and talents, and gave me high hopes for a very successful future doing whatever I wanted to do. Once a week, I wasn't the new kid, the tall girl, the anxious student who was having early-onset puberty. I was a scientist, a writer, or an artist. Whatever I wanted to do during that one day a week was exactly what I was supposed to do. They said to "follow your passion!" And "You can be a leader, a trendsetter, a success in any- and everything!" It was incredible. I wish I could bring you into that world for a minute. It wasn't really about being gifted or talented. It was about potential, having permission to try new things, hearing encouragement to be as creative and flexible in your thinking, and having support and guidance to follow our itty-bitty hearts down new roads and previously hidden paths. Every child deserves that.

Fast-forward a few decades. I would love to tell you the story of how I followed my heart into a career that was ultimately fulfilling, where I played a key role in changing the world. Perhaps I could tell a tale about an idea I had that ended up curing cancer, or a book I wrote that shattered the best-seller list and had a profound impact on global culture. Or I could spin you a yarn about my exploits in protecting a valuable resource around the world, which kept our earth from warming, and the documentary film based on said exploits that won awards at Cannes. But alas, I wrote this book instead.

With 30 years of trying to find the perfect fit, I think you'll find my stories relatable. I want to entertain you with some of my zany (or just sad) adventures in job hunting. I also want you to know that you are not alone in your job-hunting struggles. Almost everyone in our society spends some time finding work throughout their lives. Throughout this book I will offer some food for thought about the process so that by the end you feel seen and hopefully gain some insight into your own adventure. At the end, perhaps we will all relax a bit more, get to know one another, and be able to move through the hiring process with a bit more self-awareness and compassion.

Even if you're the smartest, most evolved person in your field, with advanced degrees and pages upon pages of the re-sume-worthy job experience, you can still struggle through this process. The job may seem like a perfect fit, yet at the end of it all, you're ghosted again. Or worse, after a stellar interview in which they allude to your new office, your pension and benefits, and your future with their company, you may get the dreaded form letter stating, "While we really enjoyed meeting you, we have decided to pursue other, more qualified candidates at this time."

I'm willing to bet that you have, in fact, gotten a job now and then. Maybe it wasn't the brilliant career move you had hoped for, but it was at least something that paid the bills, had benefits, and provided community. Perhaps this was a stepping stone, knowing you could work upward through the system, or at least bide your time until something more appropriate came along. I've accepted many of these jobs over the years, where the basic asks were "be a human, breathe oxygen, have the ability to type five words per minute." Please know that I feel the pain of working in limbo—it takes a long time for that to go away and can leave a scar.

Chapter 4:
Historically Speaking

I've been in the working world for a very long time. I'm a Gen-Xer, coming into adulthood during the 'grunge years' in Seattle. We first got computers in the classroom when I was a junior in high school. These were not used for much aside from learning programming languages. I was ahead of the curve on that as one of the lucky few to own a Commodore VIC-20 personal computer when I was in the 7th grade. I learned basic computer language: IF-THEN and GO-TO statements. To play video games, which I was very interested in, I connected a cassette-type player to the computer to 'upload' it. I recall telling my 7th-grade math teacher, "I want to go into computers as a career." His response, which angers me to this day, was, "Girls don't do that."

By high school, the VIC-20 was abandoned, and I leaned into sports, grades, and dating. I often imagine what my life would have been like if I had been encouraged to continue working with computers, if I could have been one of the early hires of Microsoft, retired in my 30s, living the life of a philanthropist and world traveler. I do live in the city where Microsoft is based and donate to some charities every year. Is that close enough?

For younger readers who came of age in the era when a typo could be corrected by hitting backspace on the keyboard, here is a little context on the old days. Most of us who went to college in the 1980s didn't have access to personal computers. I got a typewriter as a high school graduation gift, one of the most advanced models on the market. It had a digital reader at the top of the keyboard, so you could see a few of the words you typed before you hit "return," in essence reducing the number of errors that would need to be corrected with white-out. To do research, we spent many hours in the library using the card catalog and Dewey Decimal system to track down textbooks and journals. Formatting a resume on a typewriter was hellish, but we did it. There was no internet at this time, though early manifestations were starting to pop up, accessible in the dorm basement computer lab. I would spend a few hours there chatting online with newfound friends on ICQ. Here's a gold star if you remember that! ☆

A couple of my roommates got Macintosh computers when we were seniors in college. We were in awe of the ability to type papers and save them on a disk. Early computer games like MYST blew our minds. Sometimes we could borrow time and print our papers out at home, watching the dot matrix printer in awe. That was pretty fun. Formatting was still challenging, but it beat using a typewriter. The future was upon us!

My first jobs didn't require a resume, thankfully. We would look in the classified ads in the newspaper, or friends would tell us about job openings. The norm back then was to fill out a job application. These still exist, in nearly the same format, although we often use Adobe to fill in the forms online. Nonetheless, the questions are the same. Who are you, where are you, what is your education, and where have you worked? I filled one out two days ago. No surprises.

Due to some life circumstances, I had to pay my way through school instead of living the life of a full-ride college athlete like I'd assumed would be the case. I took on many jobs to cover tuition, room, and board. One of my early roles was working at the Pacific Science Center. I was the snake lady who did boa constrictor demonstrations, and I also blew up a lot of things in science demonstrations. I don't remember what year my last day of work was or why I left the job, but I do remember using a lot of extra explosives to really awe the crowd. Forgetting that igniting flash powder creates a lot of smoke, I inadvertently set off the fire alarms, resulting in the evacuation of the entire Science Center. When I made it to the muster point, my coworkers applauded me. After being questioned by the Fire Department about what happened, all of the firefighters sat down in the audience and made me finish my demonstration for them. I think they liked it. Talk about going out with a bang!

Since that time, there have been many jobs that I wanted to end with fire and explosions, but I've restrained myself and remained professional. Not to say I haven't tossed a few matches onto the bridges here and there. Don't worry, I'll get to that.

After graduating from college, I decided I needed a fresh start, so I moved to a rural town outside San Francisco. When I got there, I didn't have access to a computer. I remember, painfully, writing out a resume *by hand*. I formatted it nicely and used my best penmanship.

I will leave this here:

After graduating from college, I decided I needed a fresh start, so I moved to a rural town near San Francisco. When I got there, I didn't have access to a computer, and I remember, painfully, HAND-WRITING a resume! I formatted it nicely and used my best penmanship. (my cursive skills are great, too!)

Somehow, I justified to myself that this was enough. Incredibly, I did get a couple of interviews from it, but no jobs. I spent the bulk of the summer farming organic potatoes. That memory is painful to revisit and tough to share, but I think it highlights that technology was not everywhere until the mid-1990s at best. Throw some grace at those of us who struggled as times changed around us!

Having had no luck finding meaningful work, it wasn't long before I moved back to Seattle and was miraculously rehired at the job I had left. But soon I was bored and broke, and wanted a real job with real responsibility and real money. In those pre-Internet days, we found job postings in various publications such as newspapers, but mostly relied on word-of-mouth. Through a friend, I found a job that fit my skills, including the many 'soft skills' I had been acquiring while moving through an increasingly complex life.

I had a lot of confidence in my ability to do things. Most things. I still do. The list of jobs I've applied for, way back when and even as recently as last week span a wide range of skills and experience.

Despite what the title of this book might lead you to believe, I have somehow managed to get hired here and there throughout the years. Some jobs were for survival, some to build a career, while others were simply to be helpful to someone desperate for an employee. I see myself as *Unemployable* in the way that rebels see themselves as *Untamable*. I know I have more to offer and believe I have what it takes to lead–whether a company, a team, or a community group of some sort. I just don't want to have to shove my star-shaped peg into a square hole to do it. Is that so much to ask? (Don't answer that.)

Applying for jobs was pretty straightforward back in the '90s. First, we'd submit a cover letter, a resume, and sometimes a job application. By submit, I mean *mail it in.* As you can tell, the pace of job hunting was not fast. The packet would eventually be processed through whatever antiquated system they were using, and often a postcard would get mailed back saying, "We have received your application and will contact you if we want to move forward with an interview." Many times, this was the last word from a potential employer. "Pre-ghosting," I say. They didn't do a lot of phone interviews back then. This was before mobile phones, so people were generally unavailable during the day. Somehow, once in a while, interviews were scheduled. In-person was the norm in the decades before COVID, and technologies like Zoom pushed the process online. If they wanted to hire you, they would call. Remember rushing home every day to check the answering machine for job offers? No? Lucky you. Before caller ID, there would be hang-ups, mystery callers I could only assume were calling to offer me my dream job, and had moved on to the next candidate when I failed to answer. Sometimes it was a letter in the mail. It would come well after submitting materials or having the interview, and most often told me how great I was while letting me know that they were going in a different direction, continuing their search, or hiring from within. There were many reasons, each resulting in so much sadness on my part. Rejection-rejection-rejection. Yet, I kept submitting job applications and expecting different results. It's like sitting at a slot machine, knowing it's going to hit soon, just knowing it, feeding your life savings into a bottomless pit!

Fast forward to today. In many ways, everything has changed. In other ways, it's the same. I'm a serial job hunter, always scouring the internet for things that may provide a spark. First, I rework one of my 3,724,620 resumes to fit their needs. Next, I rewrite a cover letter to highlight the work and life experience I have that will bring me to the top of their pile. Often, the pile is sorted by a computer program (and, increasingly, by AI), so I utilize the technique of including all the words from the job posting to get a higher score. This often leads to a phone interview. Not always, but more often now that I've figured out how to game the system. Then it's ghosting time.

A lot of employment websites show you the status of your application. Sometimes, they forget to update, and the listing remains live for years. Once in a while, a Zoom interview is scheduled, and the real fun begins. I endure the challenge of trying to share everything good about myself in 2-D, wondering about how they see me onscreen, what they're thinking about my background, both physical location and the content of my resume and cover letter.

As I said earlier, I have a lot of confidence in myself. More often than not, I feel like I nailed the interview and expect further interviews or even job offers very soon. All too frequently, that is the end of our communication. A note may come via email saying something like, "We really liked you and were impressed by your skill set. However, we are hiring someone with more experience doing exactly what we think you're so good at." Sometimes the note comes months later, long after I've forgotten I even applied for that job. A harsh reminder that, out there, I'm still being evaluated poorly for things beyond my capacity to understand.

Section Two
Breadth vs Depth

Chapter 5:
Breadth, not Depth

I always try to find joy in any situation. It's a survival skill I had to learn early on as we moved from city to city every year or two. I had to pivot constantly, saying yes to attending the birthday party of a classmate I hadn't ever talked to or joining a team for a sport I'd never played. I quickly learned that participating without advance judgment could result in friendships. I craved these relationships and still long for them at times when I'm not involved in enough things. I also never knew when an opportunity to do something would lead to something greater, so I always said yes. I did have boundaries, thank you, when it came to things that were morally shady or illegal. Having spent a lot of my life being willing to try new things, I naturally carried that into my work life. How else would you see me holding a 30-pound boa constrictor and telling children all about how they unhinge their jaws to eat? At that job, I adopted a baby boa, named it Fluffy, and had a lot more adventures. But that's a story for another day.

There was a time when, as a social worker, I facilitated a daily meeting with a team of doctors, nurses, and therapists to discuss patient plans. At the age of 26, I already had eight years of experience talking to doctors, nurses, and therapists as part of my dad's ongoing care after he had a spinal cord injury. I knew the language. However, in this job, I was an integral part of the conversation, whereas when I was there for my dad, I was merely a participant in the meeting. No learning curve eased me into the responsibilities of the job: it was "Here you go; tell us the plan," and we ran with it. I also had regular meetings with families about really hard topics, like needing further institutional care or moving into hospice. So there I was, informing a couple of middle-aged siblings that their elderly parent needed a nursing home or was not going to get better. I'd said yes to this job, believing it would bring me career success, forgetting to look at what the job actually required of my soul.

A few zillion years ago, a colleague lent me a book called *Fuck, Yes!* The premise is that to be spiritually enlightened, you must say "Fuck, yes!" to every opportunity. It sounds crazy, but it honestly works. I still try to say yes, 35+ years later, to things that are not seriously dangerous or too expensive, or illegal. This is how I did my first triathlon, got pregnant, got on committees and boards, became a consultant, and traveled a lot. Granted, it is also how I ended up HOA President, PTSA Vice President, track coach, and more. Overall, saying "Fuck, yes!" has helped me to be active, outgoing, and brave.

My athletic career also benefited from my ability to say yes. In my early 30s, I took up cycling. I said yes to leading group rides and would lead cyclists out into the world for 20-30-40 miles at a time. It never occurred to me that I was slower or less experienced than any of them. Nobody complained, but looking back, I was clearly just winging it. I'd hop onto the front of a group during any given bike event and lead for miles, despite most of the others being men who probably thought they were stronger than me. It wasn't about my ego; I just found my pace, and others fell in behind me. One time, I remember coming out of a porta-potty midway through a cycling event, and people were pointing at me, saying, "It was HER that pulled us all here!" I was flattered. Saying yes in sports got me involved with LUNA Chix women's triathlon, and landed me a stint as a high school field event coach.

There is a term for a person who is a jack-of-all-trades, like myself. Yes, jack-of-all-trades is a term but I am talking about being a "Multipotentialite". It is defined as someone with many interests and creative pursuits. Multipotentialites don't have one core passion that drives them; they explore multiple passions, either concurrently or at different times in their life. Some argue that it is just undiagnosed ADHD, others say it is a lack of ability to commit to one thing. In any case, we are not alone! There are terms that describe so many of us–not as a diagnosis, but as a way of being that has pros as well as cons when it comes to career. One of the pros is being able to connect with others.

I have often been referred to as a connector of people, the hub in a friendship wheel, someone who knows everyone. A lot of the jobs I got called about were rooted in my hobbies. I love fitness, cycling, triathlons, running, hiking, beer, dogs, cooking, baking, writing, knitting, and theater. All of those hobbies can become jobs if you let them.

Chapter 6:
Don't Turn Hobbies Into Work

Hobbies are necessary for living a full and happy life. Don't let anyone tell you otherwise. Working 80 hours a week and then spending the rest of the time eating and sleeping is going to get you on that deathbed a lot sooner and with far more regrets. Even when you are tired, focusing on a hobby is rewarding and brings a sense of calm, peace, and hope. Sometimes it results in physical fitness, art, delicious food, happy foster dogs, or a better functioning society. There are so many ways that we need hobbies in our lives.

I grew up watching my parents take on a lot of hobbies. It was the 1970s, so it was mainly tennis, disco dancing, macrame, and jogging. After they divorced, though, my dad took his hobbies and poked and prodded them into something that would make money. He had a sports business where he spent a lot of time developing early versions of bike shorts with chamois (and unfortunately didn't patent it), along with other Lycra sporting apparel. After he died, I found two huge binders full of resumes and modeling photos he had collected from (mostly) women who I'm sure thought they were going to become successful models. Instead, they served as an early version of Tinder. He got really into rowing and then began selling recreational rowing shells, which at over $2000 each in the early 1980s, was a hard sell. He got into running, so instead of merely entering a race, he created a company and put on races. That's how I learned how to be a Race Director, a hobby-like job I've kept at for decades. Once he discovered triathlon, he started managing those as well. He liked biking, so he went ahead and organized huge weekend cycling events.

Who has two thumbs and had to volunteer at all of these events? You got it. I'm an expert volunteer. Since he wasn't willing to give up participating in his hobby, he would leave the race management to me, his teenage daughter, to go out and compete in the races.

One race I managed a couple of times involved athletes racing across Idaho's panhandle. They would start in Montana and end in Washington. The aptly named Trans-Panhandle Triathlon was a logistical nightmare, as you can imagine, since most of the race was on rivers or highways.

My role as Race Director—aside from managing the race start, water and food stops, transition areas and volunteers, plus tallying the results—was to make sure that group photos taken at the race start were developed and given out at the finish line. In the mid-1980s, this was not easy. We didn't have digital cameras, home photo printers, or any of the technology we take for granted now. I had to snap a pre-race group photo, say '*on your mark-get set-go*', start the timer in Montana, drive across Idaho to Washington, where I would then drop the film off at a One-Hour Photo developer, begging them to please please rush my order, while I set up the finish area. Once they were developed, I had to see if any turned out well enough to give out to finishers. Once that was determined, I would place the reprint order and drive east like crazy, hoping to get to the transition area before most of the athletes.

This was also one of the first times I realized that the concept of privacy goes right out the window during a race.

I recall one guy rolling up on his bike, jumping off next to his running gear, and handing me a bottle of water to hold while simultaneously peeling off his bike shorts to reveal his "swimsuit area." I was somewhere between 16 and 18 and was pretty horrified! I was not there to help people in transition; it was a case of *wrong place, wrong time* for me!

I have many more examples of this hobby-not-hobby lifestyle I was raised in. Here's one more story, then I will get back to job hunting. Since I was a child of divorce, I had visited my dad every other weekend. I was a social creature, so I often took some friends along with me. My dad was fine with this, especially on race weekends, since that meant more volunteers. One time, we were running late getting to Idaho from my home in Washington, and arrived at the last minute at the finish area of a long cycling road race. My dad was not racing this one, as it was a more regional race than the local events he usually participated in. There were five of us volunteers: Jeme', Matt, Robbie, my sister Barbie, and me. My dad ran up and said we had to record the finishers of the race in order. The race was nearly finished, and as we looked down the two-mile-long bridge they would race across to the finish line, we started to panic. These days, racers wear electronic tags on their helmets, and there is a camera available to see photo finishes. In the 1980s, it was a bunch of high schoolers standing on a couple of rocks, craning their necks to determine 1st through 20th place when a pack of 40 bike racers sped by at 30 mph. We decided to pick places by jersey colors. I would pick one through five, Matt would do six through ten, and so on. We did our best. The cyclists did not agree, unfortunately. We spent a very unpleasant afternoon sorting out the real results. Thankfully, they all helped us figure it out, teaching me an important lesson in the process: **Do not make your kids volunteer for your hobbies!**

Fast forward 30 years, and I can show you photos of my little boys handing out water at a variety of races. I didn't make them determine winners, though, or drive across the state to develop photos. Where is my medal?

Here's a cute photo of my son volunteering at a race that I was participating in back in 2012. We can't be perfect all of the time!

How does one capture the soft skills I honed in these endeavors on a resume? What about all of the other things I learned by observing (through helping) my dad's various hobbies? I can list race directing as a skill, including organizational skills, time management, and volunteer wrangling. This doesn't begin to cover what I actually had to do for all of those events, though.

Another memory just popped in. My dad promoted a local 4th of July Fun Run and got a ton of entries. I don't know who got the money, but I know it wasn't me. In any case, this was also long before computers so we would go the mailbox daily to get all of the entries, make sure they had the right amount of money written on their check (or occasionally sort the cash, since in that day people would mail cash), and then we had to sit down and fill in little boxes on every single race bib with their names, birthdates, addresses, etc. On race day, we'd stand at the finish line, pulling each serrated tag off and keeping those in order of finish that aligned with the person clicking the stopwatch every time someone crossed the line. It was a real treat. Then, imagine having to sort those into age group awards. We did that too. It wasn't exactly fun, but hey, we got a free T-shirt.

As an adult, I fell into this habit early on and can't seem to stop. I started a couple of LLCs, so at least I could group my hobby-work into a place that attempted to capture what it was that I did. I started out by getting a job doing personal care work. I did this because, in my regular life, I was swamped with helping dad hire, train, and fire a never-ending string of personal care attendants. I wanted to prove that I could do attendant work better than anyone, and also get paid. So I did that all through college, up at 5 AM every day to make sure others were able to live their lives. I forgot to live my own life a lot of the time, as is the case when you turn a hobby into work.

I, too, became a triathlete later in life. It wasn't long before I was volunteering a ton of my time to train women triathletes, sponsored by LUNA. It didn't pay, but it provided a ton of experience, which is once again hard to capture in a resume format. The soft skills of coaching new athletes to try something as epic as a triathlon encompass physical endurance and strength, emotional resilience, and trusting relationships.

I started an online group for pressure cooking long before the Instant Pot(™) was ever created. Once that came along, I transformed my hobby of posting recipes and occasionally answering questions into teaching classes on how to use the Instant Pot, as well as increasing my online presence.

This didn't pay that well; a lot of time went into promotion, ingredients, location rental, gas, etc. It was fun while it lasted, and at least I still use my Instant Pot to make yummy food. (By the way, please be on the lookout for my cookbook, which is coming out soon!) Teaching was hard. That didn't stop me from taking on a class teaching sourdough bread baking. This happened after I had taken a sourdough class and discovered that I enjoyed baking bread and, surprisingly, I was good at it, too! Through teaching, I got asked by friends and acquaintances to sell bread, so sell bread I did, followed by cinnamon rolls, scones, and more. I got a second oven installed in my home and baked my ass off during the pandemic, providing delicious sourdough to the world at a financial loss. Advertising was expensive and time-consuming. Ingredients, although simple, were expensive in the quantity that I was using. Hoping that it would bring me good karma, I kept at it for quite a while, but soon my joy of baking became my hatred of being stuck at home. Being there for the pandemic was bad enough, but having to attend to dough 24/7 was killing me. So I stopped it all. Years later, I'm still struggling to regain the lost joy of baking. If I do, I swear I will not teach or monetize it. If I were much younger, maybe I would have considered opening a bakery, having employees, and establishing boundaries between my home life and my work life. And then there is the problem with filling in that "gap" in the resume where I did so much and poured my heart and soul into it. "Taught baking and cooking classes" barely skims the surface of the time it took to do that.

There were times when my hobbies would intersect. I taught an online sourdough baking class to people who had signed up for a running race during the pandemic, as a perk. I served beer and donated cooking and baking classes to the velodrome, where, as a former track racer, I now ran the beer garden. I taught fundraising and grant writing to the PTA, where I had volunteered for many years. I coached basketball where my kids played sports. I volunteered for many years with high school theater, where my son was a thespian. I just couldn't stop giving up my time. I sometimes have a tinge of jealousy when I'm volunteering yet again and see other parents, athletes, or cooks able to relax and enjoy the experience while I'm behind the scenes prepping, setting up, organizing, tearing down, and cleaning up.

I hope anyone looking at potential job candidates, who sees a lot of volunteer experience listed, will not only pay attention to the amount of time spent volunteering, but will also ask about those soft skills that aren't immediately apparent. If they can work that hard for zero pay, just imagine what they are capable of doing when earning a livable wage and benefits!

1. What are the soft skills you have learned through activities that you enjoy?

2. What career would you have if money was not an issue?

3. Think about role models who have succeeded in non-linear career paths and do a deep dive on their life. (I will bet it seems familiar.)

Chapter 7:
Gifted AND Talented

My passion for a wide range of interests began long ago. As I mentioned earlier, I attended a program for gifted and talented youth one day a week through third grade. At this school, I was encouraged to follow my curiosity and to share what I learned with my classmates. This book is my attempt to share what I've learned with you, my fellow job-seekers, to remind you to stay curious, keep exploring, and never doubt your boundless potential.

In case you're wondering what happened after third grade, allow me to explain. We moved again, midyear, as a result of my dad's job, which relocated him every year or two. It was really great for my social life, my trust in adults, and my ability to be calm and steady. *Oh, wait, it was none of those.*

I definitely lacked consistency in my life. Cue a lifetime of anxiety as I tripped through constant and chronic new situations. We moved to a small town in Illinois and then moved again, so by the time I was in 5th grade, we were living in rural Northeastern Washington, where I attended a two-room schoolhouse for grades K-5. This was my fourth school in five years. My class of 12 was one of the largest that had gone through the school. In between the gifted school and the one-room schoolhouse, I had managed to finish the SRA

Reading Lab in its entirety. My mom always supplemented schoolwork with other workbooks, like "Finger Math" and "Gregg Shorthand" and every workbook that was ever printed. My sister and I were voracious learners and consumed them as fast as they appeared. By the time I attended the two-room school, I had already finished all of the school's available textbooks. I would spend most of the day in the reading nook with some Edgar Allen Poe or Pearl S. Buck. Other days, I would assist with teaching kindergarten. I was extremely bored and isolated. Once I entered "real" public school, for grades 6-12, I had lost my passion for learning. Despite the circumstances, I still had a lot of potential. Isn't that part of what an IQ test is for, to see if there is potential? It's not a guarantee of brilliance. Our district was one of the lowest rated in the state, so being able to say I was in honors classes (as few as there were) and amongst the high GPA graduates is not a huge flex. Thankfully, I escaped, moving across the state to Seattle for college, where I have lived ever since.

Maybe you're thinking, "At least now things are looking up!" Yeah, that would make sense, as in most tales of woe, the heroine finds her true purpose during the journey. *"Smart girl escapes her sad educational situation and becomes a success after an amazing college experience!"* Oh, boy, how I wish! At the beginning of my second quarter of college, my dad became disabled while ski racing (hobby-life strikes again). Everything changed. I now had to pay my own way through school, so I got 1-2-3 jobs at a time to survive. As you may have guessed, I have already penned a memoir about this part of my life for future publication. What should have been my time to grow and find my own way to succeed in life took a major detour instead. I stayed in school and somehow managed to graduate, only a quarter late despite many years of chaos.

Managing all of the changes that happened in my young adult life, along with having to constantly solve major problems, fostered versatility and adaptability. I didn't have the luxury of saying "no" to most things–instead, I would add each new responsibility to my list and somehow manage to make magic happen. This is where my potential shone, and I developed the confidence to try things that for most people seemed out of reach. I didn't get a chance to not do hard things, to say no, so I just plugged along doing whatever was necessary to survive. I didn't thrive, though, as I was really fucking tired. An important note-being unable to say NO is not the same as saying "Fuck, Yes!".

I got my first real job just out of college. It was a 'who you know' situation. I don't remember if I did a resume or application for that one, but I was hired as a social worker, supporting adults with developmental disabilities in the community. It was a fun job at times, a really hard job at other times, and I met some of my best lifelong friends there. At this job, I learned about time sheets, money management, expense logs, meetings, and bureaucracy. I didn't know enough to change the world yet, but damned if I didn't work my heart out and let my compassion flow into the world. I took one little break to relocate to California, and another to traipse through Europe for a few months. Both times, they let me have my job back. Looking back at it now, I realize what a gem of a place it was that supported employees as they tried out life and welcomed them back with a soft place to land. It was the true definition of work-life balance. Sadly, at the time, I did not appreciate it as much as I should have, nor was I able to get ahead financially on the low wage, so I moved on to another social work job.

That's when the reality of adulthood began to kick in. In my new job, I met some of the most amazing people who were also working to change the world, stuck in a system that didn't accept change very well. The bureaucracy of the healthcare system in this country is astounding. I learned fast and furiously how terrible it is. I also learned that being smart and helpful backfires in a large organization that will continue to pile the work on until you break. Long story short, after a lot of painful meetings, horrible interactions, and an agreement that I would quit my job in exchange for back pay and a year of insurance coverage, I found myself unemployed and without direction.

But I still had potential, right?

I didn't want to be a social worker anymore, even though I still went through the steps to get admitted into a couple of Master's in Social Work (MSW) programs. As graduate school loomed, I realized I just couldn't do it any longer, my soul having been sucked dry from the decade I had already devoted to the healthcare system. I explored some different options and soon had it narrowed down to either massage school or graduate school in Organizational Psychology. My head chose graduate school, leaving my heart's desire for massage school in the dust.

Hindsight often reminds me that massage school would have worked out better in both the short and long run. But hindsight is just that.

I floated through graduate school, one of the youngest in my program. I tried to be involved as much as I could, meeting many people while also working full-time to support myself. I was still tired, so very tired. I didn't thrive, though, as I was trying to do what I thought society expected from me instead of what I truly wanted to do. Somehow, miraculously, I graduated and now can list that Master's Degree on all 3,837,393 versions of my resume. What a win!

Amazingly, I still have potential, even now, over 25 years since I graduated. Did I live up to it? That depends on who you ask. I struggled throughout college and graduate school because of how many responsibilities I was juggling. I attributed that to the many things I had to manage, which included part of my dad's life, my own crazy life, my job, commuting, terrible anxiety, and crippling depression. Oh, and my raging, undiagnosed case of ADHD did not help matters.

I still had potential + experience. Whether that would one day equal what I saw as success was still a burning question. Why couldn't I share my experience in a way that proved that I was a capable employee? Maybe it came down to how I was perceived.

THE EXPECTATION EFFECT
What happens when society's expectations enter the picture

WITHOUT EXPECTATION   WITH EXPECTATION

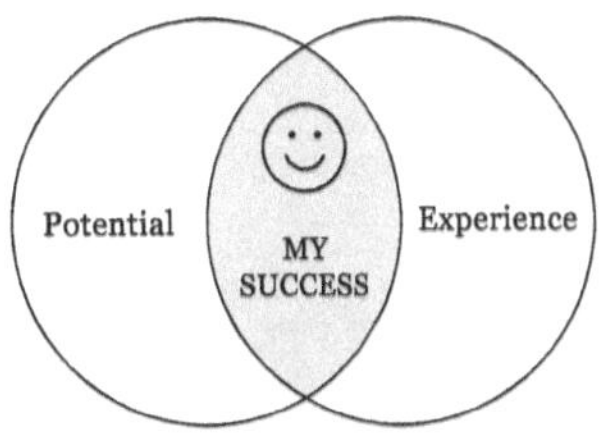

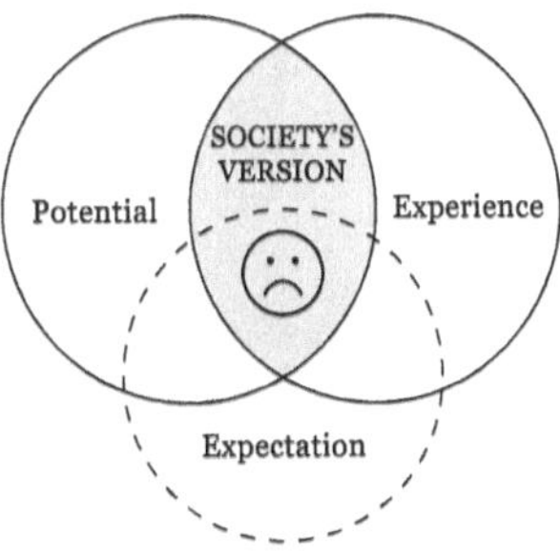

Chapter 8:
Are we really just our jobs?

"What do you do?" That is a question that comes up a lot, especially when first meeting someone. I, for one, have had to change my answer so many times that I just give a brief random answer and point at something, "Look, something shiny!" in order to change the subject. Other snappy answers: "What don't I do?" "Whatever isn't illegal in this state!" "This and that and some of the other." I have longed to be able to say that I'm a philanthropist for so long, knowing now that it is just a pipe dream. "What do you do?" is not equivalent to "who are you?" Knowing who you are and showing that in every part of your life is much more important than being able to drop a job title into a conversation. Also, "I could have been a contender!" works in some settings.

In many cases, one's identity is defined by a job. Even stay-at-home moms, after 20 years raising kids will often answer "I'm a mom but I USED TO BE A LAWYER /NURSE /PROGRAMMER /TEACHER" or whatever their job was. Insisting that we were once *important* is something we revert to automatically. It's not just moms. Many men also share past job titles or even training opportunities, like the military or being a college athlete, if they are questioned. Early experiences formed our sense of self, so to deny that and just rotely state a job title that somehow defines where on the hierarchy someone is doesn't work. We all do it and need to edit that as we go through our world.

As I have mentioned a few (hundred) times throughout this book, I have not been able to answer "what do you do?" easily. "I'm a social worker" only worked for a few years. Sometimes I would add on, "I work with adults in the community" or "I'm a geriatric specialist and do hospice work" in order to up the impressive career value. Now, I don't have any job at all, so my answer is often, "I'm a writer" hoping that will help me discuss some of my books I have written and my plan to take the publishing world by storm in my late 50s. I have also been known to say, "I do a wide variety of things, like coach high school track, bake bread and teach cooking classes while volunteering for community theatre." This is ultimately my ego piling on tasks that will give people a positive view of me, my achievements and my potential. What if we were just honest, and said, "I work a fun job doing as little as I can in order to fund my life, retire early and to help my kids get a solid footing as they reach adulthood." That rings differently to me, and is much closer to what I actually do. Well, that and "I get up, drink coffee and spend time on social media, work out, play with the dog and eventually write some words. Then later I make dinner and watch hockey." I hope nobody thinks less of me.

In theatre, I often hear actors say "I'm *just* in the ensemble." In careers, I hear people belittle their jobs saying, "I'm *just* doing customer service." I have heard athletes that I coach say, "I'm *just* junior varsity." The word **just** makes me crazy. Yes, there are times in life when we aren't living up to our potential, often taking on commitments that harken back to earlier days in order to get by. These are necessary and important roles, nonetheless. Without an ensemble there would be no musicals. Without customer service, we would be a society of angry hoarders. Without JV, learning how to excel and gain self-esteem through individual progress, there would be no sports. Everything is important. Every job that you have is important. Don't belittle what you have done or are currently doing. I don't care if your aspirations don't involve college or additional training. We all have to adult and however that is accomplished is okay by me. There are many paths to the top of a mountain. I have repeated that ad nauseum to my kids since birth!

Very few people can look back to the beginning of their work life and say that every job they've had was some esteemed title. I know that I'm still trying to figure out what I want to be when I grow up. It's not my fault that 40 years went by before I figured it out. Many circumstances result in underemployment and unemployment. That doesn't mean someone is less than another person. Being able to be okay about *who* you are rather than *what* you do is a lot easier on the soul.

It would be great if society didn't put so much value on jobs and income and if people would be able to truly follow their hearts as they made the world a better place, making enough to live a happy life and have a solid future. What I do, as someone who stumbles through the answer to that "what do you do?" question, is to ask more questions about people in order to find out more about them, instead of asking more about what they do. Perhaps that will catch on? Going forward, I challenge you to answer more honestly when you are asked what it is that you do. It can include a job but try including your life's passions, places you have been or other milestones that you are proud of besides just a job. You will find it sparks a much deeper conversation and better understanding of everyone walking around in this world we find ourselves in.

INSTEAD OF...	TRY THIS...
~~What do you do?~~	What is your favorite hobby?
~~Where do you work?~~	What type of people do you work with?
~~I'm just a nobody.~~	I love what I do.
~~What have you accomplished lately?~~	What are you proud of that has nothing to do with work?
~~Where do you go to school?~~	What's something you've taught yourself recently?
~~What do you do for a living?~~	What problem do you wish you could solve?

Section Three

The In-Between

Chapter 9:
Mind The Gap

I might have ADHD. I'm pretty sure, but I just can't get my act together to go get tested for it. Self-diagnosis seems to be a side effect of being a 'Gifted and Talented' human, and my wildly fluctuating career path does feel like a tip-off. Our culture would have us believe that most people get a job, move up a level doing more complex work, get a promotion, take on more responsibility, and perhaps become the boss or a partner in a business. Graphing from left to right, it's a simple arrow going up and to the right, all the way to retirement. Sure, sometimes there are stops and starts, maybe starting a business, getting laid off, or taking time off to have children. But those are the exception, not the norm. Right?

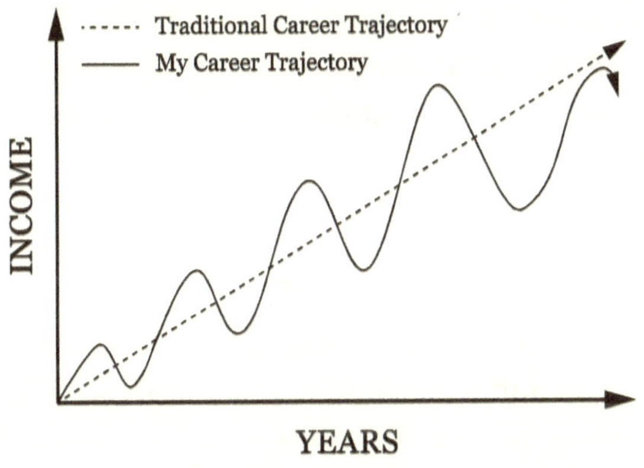

Well, my own resume (maybe yours, too?) has all of those and then some. There are jobs that overlap, skills that collide and don't make sense, businesses run and closed, clients successfully satisfied, and employers large and small. And there are the gaps. I have more gaps in my resume than a hockey goalie has in their mouth.

Those gaps don't mean I was just sitting home watching soap operas*. Finding the subtleties that exist in someone's career journey is actually the best part of interviewing potential employees. I think a lot of companies are missing out on the mystery that a wild and crazy work history can bring. Hear me out. (*OK, I confess there was a time when I spent a lot of time on the couch watching Sex and The City, but I was breastfeeding and I had nothing else I could do, because, believe me, if I could multitask while nursing, I definitely would have!)

In my case, the biggest gap was raising my kids. I did work during those years, but not always in career-related jobs and not full-time. I did, however, manage serious medical and mental health issues for my kids, took care of a disabled parent, lost a parent, moved at least four or maybe ten times, and volunteered like crazy. While it's not easy to drill down to find all that out, it's interesting once you do. I love it when people notice on my resume that I coached high school track. Or that I was a sourdough baker. The gap back in 1992? That's when I traveled Europe for a summer. 1993? That was when I was shopping around my handwritten resume in Northern California, hoping to create a new life. The gap this year? I was recovering from surgery. I didn't just lie in bed; I networked with others in my situation, created an extensive social media account about the rehab that continues to help people as they go through recovery, plus now I have an outline of another book ready to write. I think all of the little things I did in those trenches in order to survive make me a more interesting colleague. Yes, I can do the work I'm applying to do. I can also lead large groups of teenagers, put on races, raise money, and give a keynote talk at a PTA luncheon about a wide variety of topics.

When I interview, I work hard to emphasize the fact that I can do a *multitude* of things, from skills acquired during what they would consider gaps. It's often difficult to bring that up, and I swear I will find a way to highlight those soft skills better on a resume or in a cover letter. Maybe I'll write a book about just how to do it... *Wait...* (this is where I turn and slowly look at the camera, breaking the fourth wall) *I'm doing it right now!*

When you are dismissed for not having the standard career trajectory or path, or worse, screened out of consideration by AI based on dates and keywords alone, it doesn't feel good. If, on the other hand, you are given the opportunity to talk about what happened in the downtime, the in-between space, the quiet years, you'll reveal treasures untold. A question I would like to hear during an interview would be, "Tell me about a time you were doing something other than working in this field. What did you do and what did you learn from it?" That's bound to bring a more interesting and useful answer than "tell me about a time when you solved a problem at work."

I look forward to getting asked that question at my next interview. Thanks in advance for crediting me when it becomes the new HR hotness. I will add it to my resume under "things I did while I wasn't working."

Chapter 10:
Serial Applicant

I peruse one to ten job boards daily to see what openings are out there. It's a hobby for me now. Though I've been ready to give up many times, I always end up applying to one last job, *just in case*. Yes, I have a raging case of FOMO (Fear of Missing Out). Also, in case you forgot, I *am* excellent at turning hobbies into jobs, so there's that. If there was a way to get paid for applying for jobs, I would be set for life.

By now, you've probably noticed a pattern in my career path. I feel like the hunt has become a toxic habit I just can't quit. I have fallen into the compulsion zone, where applying for just about any job that checks the boxes is comforting, whether or not I really think the job is right for me.

I can apply for jobs in my sleep. Sometimes I'll get an email interview request and have no recollection of ever applying for the job. Old habits die hard. If it's a place that doesn't require me to fill out an application, I can get that sucker submitted faster than the speed of light.

At this point, I have cover letter templates for any job for which I am remotely qualified, so it's easy to quickly edit and send. And yes, one of my 9,8487,848 resumes will probably fit the bill. Some of the online job apps even hold your information on there, making it even easier to apply without much thought or effort. I'm still unclear on why companies would choose to be inundated with applicants, rather than sorting the wheat from the chaff straight out of the gate. But until someone hires me to figure it out, I suppose it'll remain a mystery.

If I ever do make the transition to full-time employee, I want to shut down all the recruiting apps and lists so I don't second-guess myself and hit apply again. If it were a dating app and we mutually decided to stop seeing other people, I would get rid of the app and not drive myself crazy swiping on what I might have missed.

As a serial job hunter, here is a typical day in my life. I wake up, have coffee, peruse job openings, walk the dogs, hem and haw, apply for jobs I may or may not want, hem and haw, forget that I applied. I might send an email about an application from a past day, or I might not. Emails arrive. I don't get hired. Repeat. I will probably have to throw my computer into a lake eventually. But in the meantime, it keeps me busy. Sometimes I read articles about employment, reinvention or resume building. I attend a fair amount of networking luncheons and support groups (via Zoom) in a variety of fields.

As George Bernard Shaw said, "Those who can, do; those who can't, teach." Let me, as your teacher, teach you that it is okay to stop applying and especially to stop looking at open jobs! The hours spent in application limbo are not productive or healthy.

Chapter 11:
The Waiting is the Hardest Part

Have you ever had to wait for the results of a medical test? Sitting by the phone, waiting to learn your fate is at the very top of the list of situations nobody wants to be in. Waiting for somebody to get back to you about a job is almost as bad. Sometimes, even worse, because the results of a job interview can change everything. Plus you may be waiting for a few different results all at once. The nervous system does not like this. At all.

For someone who has been unemployed, getting a new position can change their lives. Oftentimes, there are overdue bills, children who need things like orthodontia or even just a pair of shoes, or the means to buy healthy food. The longer someone is unemployed, the more basic needs go unmet. I've spoken before about the anticipation of getting a new job and how I personally have the problem with building it up to be the most amazing thing in the world, envisioning myself walking in on day one taking my big paycheck, paying off my bills and being able to get ahead in life for once. What my job hunting experience ultimately boils down to is that it's like playing the lottery, knowing this time, you're gonna hit it big. Then sadly you realize your chances of winning were about the same as finding a winning ticket on the ground.

It helps me to think about the people on the other end of the recruitment. I know that people in business are busy, it seems like they don't just sit there with my name on the tip of the tongue or my resume on the top of the pile waiting to call and make my day. They have all sorts of interruptions and other deadlines and lots and lots of other things going on. The more I remember this, the easier it is. But it still isn't easy.

I am going to put a bonus chapter at the end of this book that is specifically for the recruiter or other Human Resources employee who may be reading this. I am hopeful that what I put in there will change your life and everyone's life who you interact with going forward. Even if it doesn't, I am going to pretend it did so that I feel like I have done something good for the world. Once in a while you have to pat yourself on the back!

Here is a sample of what I will have for anyone dealing with the ups and downs of hiring. I know AI has taken over some of these roles, and I am truly sorry that the human touch is even harder to find nowadays. Still, I hold out hope that being more aware of your actions will pay off. There are ways to alleviate the horrible angst of waiting. First and foremost, during the application or recruitment, having even minimal contact with the applicant to let them know the timeline would be the first step. Even if it's the horrible automated email that says "we aren't going to email you unless we are interviewing you" or a simple "check our website on xxx date." Something, anything like that would make all the difference instead of having to figure out with each employer why it's taking so long, or why you never heard from them at all.

Anyone who knows me will tell you that I'm not good at waiting for things. I'm impatient in general, always thinking of what I need to be doing and planning ahead. This is not a great way to exist, but it's how I do things based on the way my life has gone, generally taking rejection very personally. It's not great, it drives both myself and those around me crazy at times. The root of this though, is hope. Despite so much rejection, I still have faith in my potential + experience. Whether that will one day equal what I see as success is still a burning question. Stay tuned...

Chapter 12:
From Small Business Owner to Employee

Many years ago, before the internet was what it is today, before Y2K, a young woman had just gotten her master's degree and was ready to take on the world. I remember being nervous and watching live New Year's Eve celebrations from across the globe, being relieved over and over that when Australia or Europe turned their calendar to 2000, the world didn't end.

Now, where was I? Oh yeah, changing my status from employee to student to intern to business owner and back to employee. I did all that during the lead-up to Y2K rearing its ugly head. I did all of those at the same time, as well, and at the end of graduate school, I had no job. I was connected to a few Wellness and Health Educators but none of them had real jobs to offer. I'd been working part-time in Medical Education for many years to pay the bills. I was contacted through a colleague about my ability to do some contract work for a big medical education company on the East Coast. I would be setting up a Medical Education testing site at a college. Having no prospects on this side of the country, I opened up my first LLC and said yes to the opportunity, successfully negotiating a salary that to date I have never matched, plus perks such as first-class airfare to go back and forth every two or three weeks. They paid for my food, lodging, and transportation as well. I lived on campus and loved the work there. It was very hard, working many long days with amazing people to get the program up and running. (Side story: a TV show was filming at the same college and we'd run into the crew now and then around campus. A few years later, I was watching Strangers With Candy, starring Steven Colbert and Amy Sedaris, and recognized their settings as the very same place that I'd been. I was so bummed that I hadn't tried harder to join their troupe and become BFFs with Amy because I know that was my destiny and I missed it!)

After my few months away, the program was operational and I found myself back home, once again unemployed. I got a couple more consulting gigs that took me to a few places in the US, then got some work I could do remotely by telephone, which was a landline back then. I tried to get more business by creating brochures, business cards, networking everywhere I could but there just was not enough work, no small thanks to a bust in the dotcom boom that had happened recently. I decided to shut it down and get a 'real' job that had regular pay, benefits and coworkers.

Decades later, I started up another LLC that encompassed my teaching and grant writing. I'm still at it, limping along. I did help someone win a $3 Million grant this year so I'm pretty good at what I do. It's really hard to keep a one-person business going at a pace that assures money is consistent and the dry spells don't happen. My current dry spell is what spurred on my job hunt this past year, once again trying to make enough money to live on. I don't care as much about the perks or about an office, but having a colleague or two would be cool, not to mention a steady paycheck and also the opportunity to work remotely. It's a tough transition, one that needs to be done very intentionally.

It's important to be realistic about what you are giving up by letting the small business go. There's the freedom, the tax write-offs, the solitude, and the appreciation of a business lunch receipt. Contrast that to what you will gain: security, money, and benefits.

Having self-employment as the bulk of experience on the resume is another major roadblock when interviewing for jobs. While self-employment allows you to do a variety of work that you love and are good at, it challenges employers to understand what it is you did for all of those years. When you happen to do a lot of different things like I do, I have had to learn to give the elevator talk to employers, highlighting my big wins and being my own champion. Employers need to remember that anyone who has been self-employed is highly creative, good at marketing, and has not made the decision to move on to work for an organization the easy way. Appreciate that they have a lot to give and that they want to give it to you. They are also probably feeling a loss of their initial hopes and dreams of running their own successful business.

The change of career paths is not always fear-driven or motivated by money. As I said before, sometimes there's a need for colleagues, perks, an actual office life and routine. Usually, it's somewhere in between the two. Life can be crazy and for myself there are times when I can take more risks and run my own business and times when I need to settle down and just work until I can free up my life again. For many years, I've had a combo of self-employment and traditional employment that met my needs. I wish that interviewers would see self-employment on a resume as a conversation starter about skills and goals and a unique way to assess whether the candidate is truly the right person for the job. In my case, I feel like I can do so much because I have been free to explore different skills, even if it doesn't look as traditional as a job that lasted ten years for one company or in one field.

Even now, when I get a job offer, I stop and take a deep look at how my business will be affected by this decision. If it's a full-time gig, is that going to take away my flexibility? Is there a remote part of the job or is it in-person? For someone who has worked from home for many, many years, having to show up in an office 40 hours a week is pretty hard to imagine. How many new outfits I would need is in itself a major factor. I have a fluid way of working that doesn't match the traditional 9-5. While I know I can do most jobs that I qualify for, I always ask myself if I truly want to do them. The older I get, the less I want to step back into a traditional 9-5 and instead do what it takes to get more clients and maybe a little part-time fun job to make ends meet. That's the beauty of being at the older end of the work spectrum. Finally, I can see that there are silver linings to age and experience! I know this sounds a bit like, "Yeah, I would like to be asked but not sure you deserve *all of this*." That's not the case, I swear, although I suppose that always saying "it's their loss" when I am rejected protects my ego.

Sometimes, to stop the insanity of job hunting, I will step back and reflect on some of the people I used to work with and work for. I also think about people who 'almost' became colleagues. It's a good way to feel productive and ponder alternative career paths. Having the knowledge and ability to track people down from the early days can be really important. Who knows, you might decide to reach out and find out how they are doing and they will have some insight on some new job prospects. Of course, I second-guess what my life would have been like if I'd been hired and stayed for my entire career in one place.

	SELF-EMPLOYMENT	FULL TIME WORK
Workplace flexibility	☐	☐
Working with colleagues	☐	☐
Employer health insurance	☐	☐
Consistent income	☐	☐
401k / retirement benefits	☐	☐
Paid holidays & sick leave	☐	☐
Schedule control	☐	☐
Tax write-offs	☐	☐
Job security	☐	☐
Professional development	☐	☐
Career advancement	☐	☐
Other benefits	☐	☐

MORE SELF-EMPLOYMENT CHECKS?

You may be built for self-employment. Independence, ownership, and control matter most to you.

MORE FULL TIME WORK CHECKS?

You may thrive in a structured environment. Stability, community, and security matter most to you.

Chapter 13:
Where are they now?

Having held on to many rejection letters, I decided to search the internet and see what happened to some of the original bearers of bad news from the early days of my job hunting. Along the way, my curiosity was piqued and I had to find out where some of the bad bosses I had ended up. This is the polar opposite of keeping up with past colleagues, as I managed to block many of them from my mind for decades, dismissing them because they were not going to be my good references, so there was no need to hang on to them.

Why do I participate in this career self-flagellation? Why did I search for people who were 'job-deniers' back in the 1990s? Mainly, I was curious if they had stayed with the organization that I had so desperately wanted to work for. As I have said before, it was my goal from early on to become employed by an organization that valued my skills and continually elevated me throughout my career. I definitely have some regrets and a big one is that I'm not able to show career longevity, nor a traditional career path to the top like so many others can. Go ahead, remind me again that comparison is the thief of joy.

Of course, in my imagination, I was hired and by now would be the *VP of Something Amazing* instead of treading water for so many years. I wondered if they had been fortunate while I continued pounding the pavement and having less than satisfying experiences throughout the next few decades. I know it's not their fault that my fantasy career(s) didn't happen. Aren't you curious now, too? Let's do a quick rundown of what I found out using a few of the old rejection letters that I have held onto for so long.

I'm not going to bog this chapter down in tiny details. If you recall, back when I was finishing graduate school, I was heavily focused on a few key places that I wanted to work–unlike today, where I will apply for just about any industry that needs my skills. Many of the people who signed the rejection letters in the late 1990s and early 2000s remained with those organizations and have moved up to top positions. Some have retired, according to LinkedIn, most from the same places. A few left and went back to that line of work again. Basically, they confirmed my suspicion that working for a few of these larger institutions where I was focused early on would have possibly made a difference in my career. That's really all I can say. Without a crystal ball, I will never know for certain if my foray into those early entry level jobs would have provided me instead with a horrible boss, abusive workplace, or if I would have had no flexibility to do some of the incredible things outside of work that I have been able to do. I hold no grudges here, it was just mere curiosity, with a side of masochism thrown in.

Next up are the bad bosses, the ones that I immediately removed from my Rolodex (it was long ago, I told you that) upon leaving the workplace. I had to track some of them down for a big, crazy background check (Chapter 29), so I spent a few extra minutes researching where their careers took them. Since those early jobs with bad bosses were many decades ago, I was not surprised to find that my old managers were in their 80s or 90s, or in some cases, dead. Others had left careers to become a psychic (who definitely should have let me know where she was when I started to look), an artist, and some had disappeared off the face of the earth, becoming truly impossible to locate. A lot of the terrible workplace experiences I had were prior to the internet. There was no virtual footprint and no shared contact information back then. Once in a while, I think of another name from way back then and do a search. It's surprisingly hard to find people if they're much older than I am. I don't know if that is a good thing or a bad thing. Some bad bosses continued their meteoric rise to the top by trampling others, which is sort of depressing.

To sum it up, from day one of serious job hunting, I was ready to commit to a long-term relationship. I wanted to work somewhere that appreciated me, that gave me regular raises and promotions and increasing responsibilities. I envisioned ending my career many decades later in a top leadership position, perhaps transitioning to becoming a board member at some point after retirement. If someone had asked me during an interview in those early days what I wanted, I would have probably said something like, "I want to work where I'm appreciated and my strengths are seen and utilized, and I want to stay here for my entire career, so long as I'm happy and doing valuable work." Nobody ever asked. It's sad. I wish that was a question in interviews. I think it would be good to try to get a read on a candidate with that angle.

Section Four
Networking

Chapter 14:
Don't Forget Where You Came From

With the wisdom I've acquired through my many years of job hunting, you would think that networking would be the very first thing I did when I started looking for work. It's so easy to get swept up in the emotion of shiny new job opportunities and forget where you came from. Sometimes, where you've been ends up being where you're going.

As long as you didn't burn the bridge when you left a job or finished volunteering somewhere, it's in your best interest to circle back and talk with someone who knows your potential at that organization about current or future opportunities. It's also valuable if your colleagues or bosses have moved on to touch base with them as well. I mention throughout this book how important it is to take care of your past relationships. It's more important than just about anything when it comes to trying to find a new position somewhere. Even in places where you may have accidentally (like the Science Center job) or purposely burned a bridge, you might be surprised if you revisit it and see what is going on and where your former colleagues are now. *There are no laws about using a voodoo doll in the comfort of your own home!*

Of course, the first lesson to learn is not to burn bridges [if you can help it]. While jobs that end uncomfortably often make us want to yell "Fuck you!" as we exit the building after a heated meeting, that doesn't do anything positive for anyone. It creates a black mark on your past, not to mention dampening morale for your coworkers. If at all possible, be the bigger person, no matter how hard that is. Do what you need to do in order to get out, don't say the words on the end of your tongue, and leave behind organized files and notes instead of dumping garbage all over your cubicle. Put that match down, sister!

Of course, I hope that bridge burning is a rare experience and that, like me, most of your last days of work have been sane and planned and organized to some extent. Nobody knows you better than the people you've worked with. They know your coping skills and have seen you reach goals. They also know your personality, your ability to be a part of a team and your passion in the field. They have seen all of your bad clothing choices and hairstyle mistakes. Back in the late 1900s, I didn't have the luxury of the internet to be able to keep in touch with people, so I had to go back and do some deep dives to find former employers and coworkers to have a list of supporters going all the way back to the dark ages. I did find them, though, at least the ones who know me and can speak for me if necessary. The good thing about going back a few decades to reconnect is that many people have moved up in the organization. Even if you left on a bad note, sometimes it helps to reconnect and share what you are doing now and see how they are. You might be surprised that they don't remember only bad things about you and perhaps shared your desire to burn bridges at that point in time. You won't know until you try.

Especially if you're early in your career, start now by keeping track of everyone you have ever met. Seriously, it is vitally important to be able to find people again. It's easier now than it used to be, with the internet and all. Since I didn't do this for a few years (decades), I have a few bosses I wouldn't be able to name even if I were being tortured. I just can't remember, and there was no reason back then to write it down in some sort of lifelong document. Do yourself a favor and keep a running tally as you move through your career(s). You don't have to stay in touch with people, necessarily, but know who they are and try to keep tabs on their whereabouts on some level as the years go by. Trust me, the years do fly by!

As I was writing this book, I was job hunting in earnest. One day, I got a newsletter from a nonprofit I had volunteered for back when they were first starting up. I volunteered for them through the pandemic, ending my time there when my own life got complicated and I had to focus on that. Still, I kept them in my periphery. When I got the newsletter, I was surprised to see they were going to add some new staff as they continued to expand. As I read the descriptions of what they needed, I was happy to see that one of the jobs described what I was looking for. Part-time, decent money, community-oriented, a company with a mission I believed in, and close to home. Not to mention requiring a lot of the soft skills that I had pertaining to volunteer management, teaching, and baking. I was thrilled and sent an email to the founder. She replied immediately, and the next day, I found myself in her office being offered the position after a synchronistic and satisfying two-hour interview. I was thrilled. I couldn't believe I'd finally found my fit, all from somewhere I used to volunteer.

I was ready to call every place that still had my resume or application open and tell them NEVER MIND, YOU TOOK TOO LONG; I FOUND THE PERFECT JOB. YOUR LOSS! Remembering that burning bridges is a bad thing, I didn't do this. It's good that I didn't because this one doesn't have the happy ending that I thought it would. Sadly, this one ended as quickly as it started, with a Monday morning email saying, with little explanation, that they had *changed their mind. 'Sorry!'* But still, the point is, by staying in touch with places I'd been, opportunities at least came my way, albeit briefly. They chose to burn the bridge. I only kept the notes.

Hopefully, you will remember to stay flexible no matter what side of job hunting you're on. If you're recruiting, run a list of your past associates through your head as well. Maybe ping a couple of former coworkers for a quick hello. You may be surprised to find they are looking for what you have to offer. I've seen this play out many times. There is no shame in working for the same organization multiple times. If, by chance, you are that rare person who holds onto old resumes from past candidates, now would be the time to reach out!

Before you turn the page to the next chapter, take a minute and sit with your thoughts. Go back to the beginning. Think about your first job: who hired you? Who trained you? Who drove you crazy in the break room? Who wrote you your first reference? Go forward from there. Every boss, every colleague, every intern you mentored, every client who became a friend. The person who took credit for your work. The one who defended you when you weren't in the room. They are all part of your network whether you have kept in touch or not. They know things about you. They remember you. And somewhere in that list is someone who could change everything.

Chapter 15:
It's Not What You Know

I know a lot of people. Looking back at my jobs, it seems that I got most, if not all of them, thanks to somebody I knew. I have gotten interviews based on my resume and cover letter, but honestly, I can't think of a single time when I cold-called a company, sent my information, and was hired (*). While it's very important to remember where you started, don't forget to connect all the dots in your life that might lead to something good.

*While writing this book, I went through the world's longest hiring process for a position at an organization where I had no personal contacts. The outcome was predictable and actually more crazy than I ever expected. The full story is just a few chapters ahead. Keep reading.

I believe that the most valuable part of job hunting is that it's very important to know who you know. Not only to know what they do in both their career and down time, but to be aware of the in-between areas where they might say, "I remember my hairdresser telling me that their sister runs a nonprofit and is looking for a grant writer."

When you are job hunting, before you create a resume, write any cover letters, or even start searching the Internet for a job, the first and most crucial thing to do is to reach out to every person you know in your world and let them know what you are interested in, when you are available, and what your superpowers are. I need to write this in ALL CAPS AND **BOLD** AND <u>UNDERLINE</u> IT! You don't need to go into the nitty-gritty–if people know you, they know you're capable of doing lots of things and will hopefully connect you to positions that are available or introduce you to people they know who might know of open jobs. A little louder for the people in the back: ***Networking is more important than any other aspect of job hunting!***

The biggest mistake I've made in my own job hunting journey was to get frustrated and discouraged, hole myself up, and just go through job postings day after day after day, sending in resumes and cover letters and doing the tests and whatever else they required, without reaching out to my contacts first. Sometimes, I'll be deep in job hunting limbo and realize I actually know somebody who works at that company, and can actually call and talk to them. In many instances, my resume has already been put where it ends up forever, usually at the bottom of the pile, because I didn't start out with an internal referral.

Since repetition increases learning, I'll repeat this here: before you do anything else in your job hunt, reach out to every person you know and ask them if they know of any positions or businesses that may be hiring. This includes people in your professional network, your social network, your family network and any other organizations that you belong to including professional groups, volunteer committees and boards. There's a ton of help out there if you reach for it. Yes, it feels vulnerable to put yourself out there, but it can save you a whole lot of time and frustration in the long run. Keep in mind that most people are very busy and they are not concerning themselves on a daily basis with how your job hunt is going. If you reach out and remind them, it's usually a no-brainer that they will help if they can.

If you happen to get a job interview without having any connections, there are still ways to make a good impression. The first thing I do is to research the company, find out who's on the board, find out who they work with on different projects and look on LinkedIn to see who I'm connected to. Note: be sure to have your settings on LinkedIn adjusted so that you aren't showing up as a 'stalker' on people's profiles. Otherwise, they may start wondering why you are clicking into their profile daily for the past month. The bottom line is: research heavily and make sure you have some sort of personal connection in your cover letter, or at the very least in an interview situation, should that come to pass. At a minimum, they'll see that you've done your homework to find out more about their company and can speak from a place of knowledge, rather than just listening passively in an interview.

There are a couple of places I've always wanted to work. One is a local university, where I not only went to school for my undergraduate degree, rowed on the crew team, and worked as a part time employee in another department for over 10 years, but also worked at a related affiliate for a few years. I knew quite a few people in the organization and felt like I had enough experience and connection to get interviews. Early on, I would write letter after letter about jobs and get rejected immediately, only *once* getting a phone call, but no interview. I have no idea why I just can't get my foot in that door. I suppose I should take it as a sign that it's not the right fit for me. Rejection is protection. Still, I can't help but look at their hiring webpage and see that I'm qualified for a number of jobs and of course have to go ahead and apply for them because of my aforementioned application addiction. Interestingly, I did get contacted recently through a professional contact about a contract job there. After a vigorous (all Zoom) interview process, they went with someone else. Later, though, they did contact me about doing some hourly work for them, so it's not a lost cause. Maybe we'll revisit this in book 2, '*Employable!*' For now I will use this as a learning experience in which I should have created a stronger network over the years.

Back when I was fresh out of graduate school, when dot-com businesses were thriving, I was doing consultation for work-life programs and health education and had contracts here and there. None of them were full-time or giving me what I saw as my own work-life balance. One very cool company where one of my friends worked took great care of their employees. I wanted to work there so badly. I went along with my friend to many of their social events, and got to know a lot of the employees. I even hung out in the common areas at lunch on occasion sometimes, just because I could (this was before security was crazy like it is today). Sadly, no job was ever available that was within my skillset, which frustrated me so badly because I knew if I could just get into that company, I would be thriving and so would they. Eventually, I let that one go and realized it was not for me.

Unrequited job-lust is a hard pill to swallow. Of course I feel like the solution would've been for both my friend and human resources to recognize that there was an (amazing, remarkable, smart, brilliant, fun) person available who could do great things. They would find me a job, one that I was able to produce a ton of great programming help related to employee retention, employee happiness, and work-life balance. These were all things I professed to be my true passion after I finished graduate school with a degree in Organizational Psychology and Workplace Wellness. If you are in a situation where you can see the same person's resume coming up for multiple jobs over a long period of time, it should be mandatory to talk to that person and see why they want to work there. It could be a game-changer! Hiring someone that is already passionate about the organization or the work is a win!

The fact that I'm writing this book after over 30 years of intensive job hunting and continual rejection is, in a word, painful. Hopefully you will use these stories, tips, and tricks to land your ideal job, and it will have all been worth it. It's the ultimate philanthropy. From a martyr who sacrificed everything to gather data: *You're welcome!*

WHO ARE YOU FORGETTING?
A few questions worth sitting with

SCHOOL	Who sat next to you on your first day and never left your side?
WORK	Who taught you everything about what no to do, and saved you years of mistakes?
VOLUNTEER	Who stood beside you for a cause, not a paycheck, and showed you what commitment looks like?
NEIGHBORS	Who knew your name without being told, and watched out for you without being asked?
FAITH COMMUNITY	Who offered you grace on days you didn't deserve it?
SPORTS & FITNESS	Who pushed you past the point where you would have stopped on your own?
HOBBIES & CLUBS	Who saw the part of you that work never could, and loved that version best?

Your network is not a list. It is every person who ever changed the direction of your day.

Chapter 16:
The Care and Feeding of References

I spend a great deal of time editing each version of my resume, writing a personal, exciting cover letter, and then, of course, shopping for the interview outfit and shoes. I'm so prepared when the big day comes. There have been moments when I thought I was getting a job offer, and references were being called. Then, suddenly, here comes the rejection, completely out of left field. Don't forget to keep your references on your side. While we often think people are on our side and gung-ho for us to be gainfully employed, things can happen that change their view of us, destroying our chances of getting hired.

References are the last bastion of 'truth' that a potential employer hears. There are rules in place for what is legal to ask as well as answer, but we all know that these boundaries often flex. Late in the game, a bad reference can screw up a job offer, which can mean no income, benefits, food on the table, or ability to pay rent. It is imperative that the applicant review who is speaking on their behalf before submitting their name.

Finding out that a reference has soured on you can shock you to the core and cause you to question everything you know, wondering what you did to mess up that relationship and if other references are not being advocates either. It can rock your world in a bad way to discover this is the reason you did not get a job.

As you go through your references, be sure to network authentically with them. The care and feeding of them is important, and if you find you have to be fake-nice to keep them on your side, perhaps replacing them is the best option. It's an important skill to have for anyone navigating their career – as you decide that someone would be a great reference, be sure to ask their permission and keep that relationship up to date.

In my case, I had a really good friend I'd made through work. We socialized outside of work, volunteered in the community and participated in similar activities while we worked together and for a few years after that. It seemed like an authentic, healthy friendship with a link to professional work. I used them often as a reference, with their permission. Unbeknownst to me, they got tired of me for some still unknown reason. Instead of reaching out, they just went dark. And as friendships do, ours faded. I still had them written down as a reference. At one point, I applied and interviewed for a job and, ironically, one of my friends in that organization was charged with checking my references.

He called me one day with an alarm in his voice. "Did you know that [Friend X] is saying very negative things about you? I asked an assortment of questions about you, and every single answer was tinged with jealousy and anger, showing you as a bad candidate." I was aghast. Over 20 years later, I still can't wrap my head around someone doing that to me. My calls to them went unanswered. We never spoke again, and I removed them from my reference list immediately.

Take it from me—don't take anyone for granted you assume is on your side. Nurture that relationship and make sure they know when you are interviewing and when they may be contacted about certain positions. They are free to say what they will, but it's best to know if what they are saying is so horrible that you are losing out on job opportunities.

Chapter 17:
Scammalammadingdong

Being a serial job hunter, it is second nature to click on different opportunities, only to discover myself filling out and submitting what I thought was a job application, finding out that I have just sent my personal information to a data farmer or sales site. It's buyer beware–you must read the fine print before hitting send, which is easier said than done. In the flurry of my stop-and-go job hunting strategy, it's inevitable that using automatic, robotic application processes results in mistakes. Luckily, I haven't had my identity stolen or my bank account emptied. Yet. But I'm sure my job history is easily findable on the dark web, just in case someone wants to explore what it's like to struggle with work satisfaction for decades (and go on to write a *best-selling* book about it).

These websites have used my information to send me offers on a great deal of things that would ostensibly make my life better. One of the exciting opportunities I'm sent on a regular basis is the chance to have my resume reviewed by an actual professional in the resume writing field. No strings attached, except for all of the strings. My mama says if it's too good to be true, then it isn't true. While it *is* true that everyone should have their resume looked at by people who can make suggestions for improvement, you shouldn't have to be constantly solicited by a predatory app about it. If you are me, you already have 3,588,366 varieties at hand, all of which have been edited, polished and saved as a PDF for just the right occasion. I don't need to send my money to someone to look at these versions. Especially now that the process is becoming more automated and it's often more about what words are included instead of how it looks. By the time a human is looking at it, you are probably on the interview list already, so your carefully formatted columns and bullet points are not as necessary as they once were.

Next up on the list of popular ways people attempt to take my money and improve my work life are certifications and courses. I get at least one message on LinkedIn every day about a certification or course that will not only make me more employable than my competition but will also increase my knowledge of a field I'm already pretty competent in. And not only one course, mind you, but a *series* of courses. Certification can be a good thing, but if you're looking at dropping a few thousand on an online certificate, it's of the utmost importance to do a quick look-see if it's actually valued on the job market.

And by the way, *no*, I do *not* want to buy a damn franchise!

Besides certificates and courses, I'm often invited to apply for a variety of degree programs at universities around the world, mostly online. While it's true that I would love an assortment of advanced degrees, the reality is that I'm barreling toward 60 with two kids in college and a lifestyle that matches my odd-job income. I'm not sure taking on $50-100K in debt right now is the best thing for me. There's not enough time to pay back a student loan and make enough money before I'm ready to retire. Thanks for asking, though.

Occasionally I will click through some job posting to an application and will automatically start filling it in, clicking boxes, for example:

EMPLOYMENT APPLICATION

Please complete all fields. Or Don't. Nobody's reading this.

APPLICANT DEMOGRAPHICS

☑ White ☑ Female ☑ Old ☐ Single

☑ Kicked him to the curb ☑ Married to the mob

☑ Gen X ☐ Millennial ☐ Boomer

EDUCATION

☑ Master's Degree ☐ Bachelor's Degree ☐ Associate's Degree

Blood Type: ☐ A+ ☐ B+ ☐ O- ☐ AB- ☐ Other: ___________

EMPLOYMENT PREFERENCES

Salary Desired: ___________ *(lol)*

☑ Remote ☐ Full-Time ☑ Part-Time ☐ Contract

☐ Legally authorized to work in this country

☐ Require sponsorship for employment visa

☑ Would prefer to live anywhere but here

SUPPLEMENTAL INFORMATION *(REQUIRED BY THE UNIVERSE)*

Firstborn Child's Name: ___________________________

Sun / Rising / Moon Sign: ___________________________

Aura Color: ___________________________

Spirit Animal: ___________________________

Hogwarts House: ___________________________

Phobias (check all that apply):

☐ Spiders ☐ Accountants ☐ The Truth ☐ Clowns

Greatest shame: ___________________________
Limit 141 characters. Yes, one more than a tweet. We want just a little extra.

Relationship with Gravity:

☐ Stable ☐ It's Complicated ☐ In Denial

Suspicion re: "Birds" (1 = They Are Real • 10 = Surveillance Drones):

☐ 1 ☐ 2 ☐ 3 ☐ 4 ☐ 5 ☐ 6 ☐ 7 ☐ 8 ☐ 9 ☐ 10

Are you now, or have you ever been, a member of the Reptilian Elite?

☐ Yes ☐ No ☐ Prefer not to say

☐ I certify that I am not currently a hologram.

☐ I agree to have my internal monologue monitored.

This is followed by rapidly autofilling my home address, email and phone and then suddenly realizing that what I'm being asked is above and beyond the norm. Thankfully, I have learned quickly what happens from sending in these dubious applications. They don't get me job interviews, but they do get me on mailing lists that result in a lot of spam. I have since gotten better at applying the brakes and stepping back to look more thoroughly at what I'm being asked.

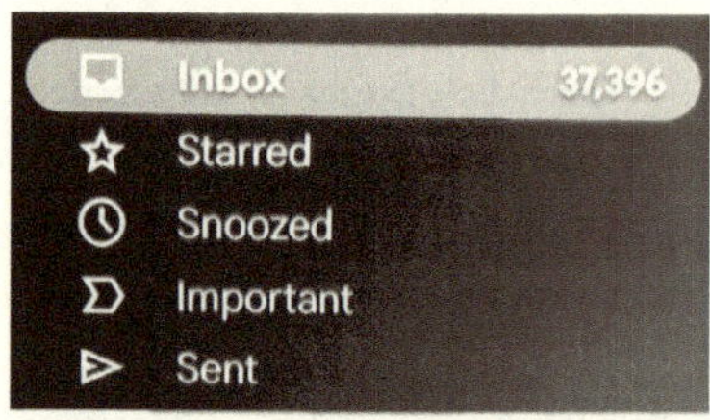

If I look at the number of unread emails in my inbox, I tend to freak out. It can be in the tens of thousands at times. I do an occasional purge, but it always fills up so fast. In fact, right now I have 37,396 unread emails. Who has time for that? Many of them are the result of applying for what I thought were jobs, but were really ways to get information sent to me constantly about a product that will increase my success with job hunting. If only my job was blocking and unsubscribing from unwanted emails, I would be rich.

If you're bleary-eyed, please go get some fresh air, coffee, play with your dog, ride your bike or run an errand. Step away from the computer! If any part of an online application seems off, *don't send anything*. If there is a link to enter information, go to the main website to check if there is actually a job open there. Ask yourself if you're just playing the application game. Breathe, step back, and be a bit more mindful. Maybe read a funny book about job hunting and recommend it to your friends, family, and colleagues! Ooh, yes, do that!

Chapter 18:
Your Reputation Precedes You

From my very earliest jobs to my most recent gig, most have been secured in non-traditional ways. In fact, when I sit and reflect on all the jobs I've ever landed, none of them were from sending someone a letter and resume and nailing an interview. I guess I need to rethink my current job-hunting strategy! One of the ways I've found myself employed is through reputation. Yes, reputation. I have a good one, at least, since nobody is asking me to deliver unmarked packages to nefarious meetings or swallow drugs to transport across international waters. Just the opposite: I have been sought out by employers who heard of me from someone I know or have worked with.

I have a lot of friends, and I strive to be an excellent friend. I will answer texts and emails and show up on time when we have a plan. I will have your back. Secrets stay secret. That's how I keep adding to my friendships. I don't sway because, at the core, that's who I am. Sometimes, when people are looking for an employee, and usually in a more desperate or emergent timeline, I will get a call or email or text saying, "Hi, so-and-so told me that you were really great at (insert amazing thing here). We have been looking for someone with your skills here at Company X and wonder if you are available to talk more about this?"

It always catches me off guard when this happens. I'm immediately flattered because it's like being set up on a blind date—your friend thinks you're so great that you should meet this other party. But it's different from a blind date in that this other party is ready for marriage. Immediately. Not one to take my time jumping into serious relationships, I have gone forth in most of these situations, taking jobs that maybe don't feel like a perfect fit, but, hey, they think I'm marriage material, so why not?

Usually, there's a period of time in which I can do research on the job before I commit to a new workplace, or in some cases, a new career. Sometimes, though, I get asked to take a job in a shorter and less informed timeline than I would prefer. I know in my heart that at the root of the job is desperation because of some situation where the right person cannot be located—whether it is a really tough position, bad hours, lack of money or benefits, or even a way-too-long commute.

My advice is to listen deeply when you are being touted as the best person for a job you were not aware of until they called you. Trust that gut instinct. Not all of these jobs for which I have been romanced have been bad. Some of them were just not the perfect fit that was promised. In my own defense, many times I was in a situation where I was looking hard for work (which for me seems to be all of the damn time), and was myself a little desperate. There may have been a lapse in hearing any positive feedback for a while, so having someone pop up out of the blue saying they heard great things about me is also going to get my attention.

In the early years, those jobs were not full-time career gigs. Often, it was merely one caregiver-type position, moving on to another client, or working with the public and moving to a different customer service role. As I have gotten older, the jobs have changed a bit. There are still a few where I was asked, maybe out of desperation, but I like to think it was because of my amazing personality and customer service skills that allowed me to thrive at selling beer or costumes.

The pandemic changed job hunting as much as it changed working, so to get a call at that time about a job that needed me was definitely flattering. It was during one of the worst weeks of my life that I stumbled through the introductions, interviews, and job acceptance while the rest of my life and the world were imploding. My gut said not to do it, but the promise of money and benefits in a new-to-me industry lured me in. *Golly gee, they really like me, so let's do it!* Life continued to crumble, the pandemic kept pandemicking, and the job did not end up full-time, nor did it provide the much-needed benefits I was hoping to receive for my time. I liked the place and the people, but the timing was terrible. My dad got very sick, leaving me to manage his decline and eventual death, so I pulled the plug. No, no, not on my dad! On the job. I couldn't make it fit with how crazy my life had gotten. It was tough to establish that boundary because the work was not bad and the people were great. Still, I just wasn't there emotionally. A few times in the following years, I was asked if I would like the job back, which was again greatly flattering, but with more terrible timing in a different period of my life that was just terrible in general.

Another call came in about a year after I'd left the last one. This time, they told me how excited (desperate) they were for me to come on board as a high school coach. I wasn't sure about taking it, as I knew life was beating me up, but it was a way to get out of the house into the fresh air and be in charge of something good. My gut said *wait*, but they were in a hurry. So I said yes. A rebound employment, so to speak. Every year, I questioned whether to keep this job. I'd gone through divorce, moving, terrible physical ailments, awful weather, surgery, and more, and somehow managed to work, and do it well. Then, almost like they knew I was writing a book about my job experiences, they opted not to rehire me and instead ghosted me. It was a rather abrupt ending to my years as a high school field event coach. My ego is still a bit bruised from that whole ordeal.

The last word looks different every time. Whether it is a post mortem email to a coaching staff, a well-timed comment before a hiring decision, or calling out an interview process faux pas so it doesn't define you. That last story fills an entire section of this book, so keep reading and soon you get to learn a lot about some pretty crazy hiring practices. In the meantime, let's drill down into interviews. I guarantee I have had things happen that are unique to me, as well as things that seemingly happen all the time to everyone.

Interviews

Chapter 19:
Work It, Girl!

Once in a while, we all take risks. Sometimes, these risks are so far outside of our comfort zone that it is impossible to wrap our heads around them at the moment. In college, my dad called and said he had a friend who could set me up on a tryout to be a model at the Bon Marche. Back then, the Bon was a big deal, a huge department store in Seattle. I can even sing the theme song, "Day-O, One Day Sale, One Day Only At The Bon Marche!". I can't remember the details, but I know I almost hyperventilated thinking about doing something that put my body on display like that. When I was 20, I was a self-conscious, sweaty, pasty, out-of-shape smoker with dyed-black hair who partied instead of sleeping. I had a lot going on in my life, but self-care was not on the list.

Despite my extreme aversion to this opportunity, I did what my dad said and went down to the Bon Marche to try out to be a model. They wanted a headshot, but the only picture I had was a 3 x 5 of my high school senior picture. On the back, I scrawled my name and phone number with a borrowed Bic pen. I waited in the hallway in a long line full of actual models. Their long, thin bodies and chiseled faces, with long flowing hair and carefully applied makeup was very intimidating. I couldn't breathe; my anxiety was outside of my control. I almost left multiple times, but my legs would not obey, so I remained in line. Soon the line of models, and myself, filed into a large room with a runway. I had no choice but to finish this.

My shaking hand reached out to give them my 'head-shot'. They looked at me quizzically, shrugged, and handed me a jacket, telling me to "put it on, walk the runway, take it off, do a turn, and walk back". It seemed simple. My rapidly tunneling vision became one small point of light at the very end of the walkway. My ears were ringing so loudly I could barely hear the music, which was, if I recall, Straight Up by Paula Abdul. As I took a deep breath, held back my tears, and did what I thought was my best modeling strut, trying to channel Cindy Crawford. I awkwardly took the jacket off at the end of the runway and turned around, probably look-ing more like a malfunctioning robot than I did a model. I attempted to throw the jacket casually over my shoulder, hooking it on my hoop earring in the process. I then dragged my sorry ass back down to where the people in charge sat with their jaws on the floor. I set the jacket down, said thank you, and walked out of there as fast as I could. I swore I would never do anything like that again. But of course, I did just that in other ways throughout my life, with no regrets.

This Girl Worked It!

Chapter 20:
First Impressions

Confession time. As is obvious from my short career as a would-be model, I worry a lot about how I look and how people perceive me. A lot of this comes from growing up as a tall, strong, athletic woman in a world that really didn't make space for that. I feel like today it is better for girls in my (size 10) shoes, although I suspect it isn't all rainbows either. I have always been hyper-paranoid about how I appear to others, assuming the worst. This gets me all worked up on interview day about my hair, clothing, jewelry, accessories, demeanor, etc. I know it is ridiculous, yet it makes me spiral way too often. After all, as I wrote earlier, I'm now older, grayer, softer, and much more invisible in general. Nobody cares what I'm wearing. The older I get, the more I'm able to focus on the words coming out of my mouth, rather than how I look.

Having known people with much more prominent DEI traits, I feel like those dealing with abject racism and discrimination (e.g., for being gay, for being trans, or for having a permanent disability) have many more barriers than I do as a grey-haired, middle-class, white female. I feel for anyone who leaves an interview feeling less-than, or who doesn't get hired for a reason that just doesn't sit right.

Most people will not admit that they notice the appearance of job candidates. But how can you not? I've done it when being interviewed by a group. Going around a room, I make a snap judgment of the people on the team. I guess at who they are and what role they play socially or professionally. I'm usually dead wrong.

Let's shake up this book a bit with an experiment! These days, we can put a list of job requirements into AI, and it will spit out a picture of a perfect candidate. For this experiment, I used a job posting that I found on Indeed, one that I would definitely (and did) apply for.

"We're seeking an experienced grant writer with a strong track record of securing funding for nonprofits across government, foundation, corporate, and individual sources. The ideal candidate can identify new opportunities, craft compelling and impact-driven proposals, collaborate with program staff on budgets and narratives, manage multiple deadlines, and handle grant reporting with precision. This role requires excellent communication skills, attention to detail, relationship-building with funders, and comfort working in a fast-paced, mission-driven environment. A relevant degree, experience with grant management systems, and demonstrated fundraising success are preferred."

First, I asked AI to 'create images of a grant writer based on the [attached] job description'. Of the four pictures it rendered, three were men —two of them men of color. The sole female was white and younger, but was wearing glasses because she must be smart.

Next, I asked AI to 'generate four photos of older female grant writers', and they went with much, much, much older women, more akin to a reboot of the Golden Girls. I didn't identify with any of them.

My final search was to 'show me grey-haired grant writers', and the resulting four images were of men, all of them with beards.

Based on the job hunting results I have had this year, I have to assume that AI was doing the hiring and that I simply didn't tick their boxes. Maybe if I grow out this menopause-given facial hair, it will give me a leg up in my next interview?

The takeaway is that you never know what preconceived assumptions a hiring team may have about their candidates. All we can do is go in representing ourselves honestly and with the knowledge that we have what it takes to do the job. How we look is just an aside.

Chapter 21:
Work For Free!

I've helped numerous friends and colleagues with their startups, pro bono. Starting a business is high risk, costs a zillion dollars to get things rolling, and is often terrifying because there is no income for months or even years while things get going. It sucks to try to succeed in the world. I don't mind, once in a while, offering advice or even writing a few grants here and there to try to bring in some funding. It's kind of like being a massage therapist and once in a while you give your partner a foot massage to keep them happy just because you can (and because they made dinner and did dishes so it's the least you can do) and it's not making a dent in your profits.

My head spins when I look at the jobs that websites like LinkedIn send me, with a huge list of Grant Writer positions. So many of them sound great until you see the word *volunteer* embedded in the description. I didn't spend years and years perfecting my grant writing techniques in order to donate all my time to a company. I get it, they don't have funding and need it. I could write a book about how backwards our society is, making the agencies that ensure safe living raise their own money while simultaneously providing life-saving services to those in need.

I do love volunteering. There's something so joyful about it because there are no strings attached. I'm there because I want to be. I'm doing good things. I'm helping people get their needs met. I can sleep at night. However, I like to volunteer on my own terms and have learned over many years that I can say no. People always, always, always need help, and there is no shortage of ways to give back. I over-volunteered for too long and finally learned that lesson. I get a bit irritated these days, after spending many years honing my professional skills, only to see that so many of the postings for jobs are for volunteer positions.

I wonder if other careers have this same issue? While voluntary medical work exists (e.g., Doctors Without Borders), I doubt that when an MD reviews a list of jobs they could apply for, half the jobs don't offer a salary, just a small stipend for their time, if that.

The same goes for being a member of a board, which consumes a ton of time. I get a lot of ads for volunteer board membership for things I have never heard of, and wonder who they're targeting with this. It's usually a pretty specific person who is asked to be on a board for something, with skills, experience, and connections specific to that organization. So no, I don't want to apply to be a volunteer board member for some natural gas company in North Dakota, thanks all the same.

All I've ever wanted to do with my life is to make the world a better place. If I based my career on what LinkedIn shares with me, it seems like the main way I can accomplish this is to work for free. The only thing missing is my ability to pay for my home, food, and such. I guess I can go without, right? Umm, not quite. While my dream has been to be a philanthropist, I haven't quite made it to the top 1% (nowhere close!). The scary funny sad thing is, I have a feeling that if I went ahead and applied for any of these non-paying positions, I would still get rejected.

Tangent time. I'm going to take a minute to rant just a little bit more about the problem I see with the nonprofit financial structure in our society. In order to do good, whoever starts the nonprofit must be willing to work for free for months, years, or decades in order to get enough history to allow them to finally apply for funding. This is so upside down. I can't tell you how many times I've tried to help startup nonprofits get funding and been rejected because they are "too new.' So how is it even possible to make a difference? Thankfully, it happens. Mostly through years of persistence by people who are goodhearted, sticking to their guns and doing things that matter. It should not be so difficult to make a difference in our world. We should all have our needs met, attend to our communities, and have the right to feel safe and well.

With no further ado, here is my 100% free advice to anyone starting a nonprofit that is struggling to get funding. Seriously this is 100% free for you! Be creative. Could it be a ramp-up? Request the first month's services for free and then start paying for hourly work? Perhaps reach out to grant writing certification courses and get some students to do the work as a part of their education, instead of looking for seasoned professionals to stop job hunting and start working for free. There are ways that still allow the good guys to succeed without devaluing the career of those people who have worked for so long to perfect what they do. One thing I do highly recommend is hiring a contract grant writer for a month (or more, depending on needs). They can help get things headed in the right direction. Sometimes a little nudge and organization is all it takes. Just in case you are in this situation, I am going to post a graphic to highlight how useful this could be. For other types of work, a consultant hired short term can really help align your needs and goals. I could write a book about how to start a nonprofit, but in the meantime, here is the information I promised.

BEFORE YOU HIRE A GRANT WRITER

How to maximize one month of a grant writer's services:

☐ 12-month grants prospect calendar with target grant deadlines

☐ Outline of a narrative library for ongoing grant use

☐ Links to potential funders relevant to your mission

☐ Outline of an LOI that can be adapted for various opportunities

☐ Needs assessment narrative for ongoing grants

☐ Submit one completed grant application

Infrastructure and planning helps guide future success.

Chapter 22:
Job Search Websites and Apps

Thanks to rampant gamification, job search sites can be oddly addictive. I get emails many times a day from LinkedIn that herald new and glorious jobs in things such as Grant Writing, Healthcare Administration, and, strangely enough, CEO. Apparently, LinkedIn, like my 3rd grade teacher, is convinced that I'm CEO material. *Tell me about it, LinkedIn!*

I've found sites like Indeed to be the easiest to use, despite its many flaws (which I'll get to shortly). There are also sites for high-paying jobs (Ladders), remote work (FlexJobs), and others like ZipRecruiter or Monster that have been around for a while.

It's easy to get sucked down a search rabbit hole. Digging ever deeper, entering more keywords, former employers, job titles, and discovering hundreds of jobs I'm sure I'm perfect for. Never mind that I would have to move to Kentucky or New Mexico, or that I need a few extra certifications to be one of the top candidates. My brain always tries to convince me to apply-apply-apply.

Most often, these applications simply vanish into thin air. I've recently given up on bulk applications, since I rarely hear a peep from any of them, with the exception of Indeed and Government Jobs. Since Government Jobs

tracks the resumes, I can watch my application be rejected on their website in real time. I've actually gotten a few
interviews from GovermentJobs.com. In fact, Chapter 29
tells a real doozy of a story that began there, so you've got
that look forward to. Keep reading.

I've learned to become a bit more rigorous in exploring open positions sent from apps. In the past, I would
click 'apply', do what they asked (of course, rewriting a
zillionth resume and cover letter focused on the needs of
the job), and wait and wait, ultimately hearing nothing.
Sometimes, there would be an email saying my resume
was received. Usually, if there was an email about this, it
also had a sentence saying they are receiving an ungodly
number of applications, so don't expect to hear anything,
ever. I do believe that many of these are just data mining
for resumes. I wish I understood just why they needed to
do this. What is gathering my lowly information going to
do to make their recruiter's jobs easier? Of course, my first
assumption is money—somewhere, somebody is making
money off the sheer number of applications or resumes
that are sent in. But why else? I did a quick evidence
search, and here's what I discovered.

Increasingly, companies are using automated resume
reviews to speed up screening and streamline the recruitment process. This is what forces us to adapt our resumes
and cover letters for each application. Maybe I should just
copy and paste the job description directly into my resume? Supposedly, this automated keyword search makes
it easier to identify top candidates. What it actually identi-
fies is people who know how to copy-paste keywords.

The other claim is that it reduces bias since it focuses
on experience matching rather than personal characteris-
tics. But, as it turns out, it does exactly the opposite. When
computers screen for the qualities of top candidates, they

compare them to existing employees who've excelled in those positions, most of whom are—*surprise, surprise*—straight white males who graduated from prestigious universities. AI and DEI, as it turns out, don't mix.

The actual experience of using these recruiting apps to apply for a job is a lot like shopping on overseas sites like Temu. The offerings are vast and tempting, but there's a lot of lag time and the results are inevitably disappointing. The one semi-useful feature they offer is a tracker within the applicant profile that allows the applicant to see their application status on the jobs they've applied for. Of the ten or so I've applied for in the past few months, most still say "application received" or "in review." A few of the jobs are closed. Some still say "screening interview scheduled" when actually, said interview was held months ago, and that was the last I heard from them. I am still waiting for one of them to say "offer accepted!" My workaround to submitting to jobs on Indeed or LinkedIn has been to see a job post and, rather than submitting in that app, go directly to the company's website and apply for it there. Sometimes it works, other times they just redirect you back to the app. I've learned that most of those redirect jobs are the ones that don't ever respond. There is rarely a way to contact anyone about the status of an application, or the outcome of an interview, when you use the apps. They have a screening middleman in many cases, who cannot share any relevant information. This is what comes of taking the humans out of Human Resources.

As I keep reminding you for some reason (apparently I really enjoy dating myself) back in the 1990s, it was harder to find open jobs because there was no internet and there were no websites. As the internet began to impact our world, listservs got more popular as a way to job hunt, alongside the tried-and-true method of *networking*, which remains the number one way to find a job.

By the way, if someone I know would like to hire me and confirm my hypothesis about networking, call me. I'm available.

JOB SEARCH SITES, REVIEWED
An honest assessment

Indeed	The Internet's largest job black hole. You apply to hundreds. You hear back from none. Occasionally rejects you for jobs you never applied for.
LinkedIn	Less a job site, more a place where people announce they are "humbled and excited." Also where you discover who got your job.
Glassdoor	Where you read anonymous reviews warning you not to take a job six months after you already took it.
ZipRecruiter	Their tagline is literally "Applying is easy. Hearing back isn't." At least someone is being honest.
Monster	The original. Still alive. Like that one coworker who survived every single round of layoffs and nobody knows why.
FlexJobs	Charges you a subscription fee to find a job. The only site that screens out scams, which tells you everything you need to know about every other site.
The Ladders	Only lists six-figure jobs. For when you want to feel simultaneously aspirational and completely depressed.
USAJOBS	The federal government's job site. Requires a 47-step application and the patience of a monk. Position may no longer exist by the time you finish.
Government Jobs	See Chapter 29. All of it. Every single word.
Craigslist	Still technically a job site. Also where you can find a used couch and a conspiracy theory in the same afternoon.

Chapter 23:
Homework and Testing

Understandably, certain careers require proof that you can actually do the work. If you're a software engineer, for example, you would expect some sort of test or sample project to prove that you can, in fact, write code. As a grant writer, it definitely makes sense that an employer would want to read some of the past grants I've written and hear about the funding I've secured. No problem. What bothers me is being asked to take a test of some sort *within the interview process.* Especially when it has nothing to do with my capacity to do the job for which I'm interviewing.

I've been asked to take a typing test, a math test, a test about alphabetizing and filing, and even to create Power-Point presentations. Nothing will convince me more thoroughly that this is not the job for me. Maybe that seems stuck up or elitist, but after all my years of writing and multiple degrees, I draw the line at being asked to prove that I know the alphabet by heart. (OK, sometimes I do have to sing the song in my head, I am human!) I have gone through with some of the testing because it can be awkward to simply get up and walk away. Once, I was sat down in a room at a computer and told to "just answer the questions." What popped up was a typing test and a basic math test. I felt like I'd been tricked into taking the most boring, unchallenging version of the SAT. If you are interviewing a professional with plenty of education, please reconsider asking them to jump through insultingly basic hoops.

Even grant writing samples can be treacherous. One nonprofit sent me a sample Request For Proposal (RFP) for a grant and asked me to fill it out. When I asked for more information on the narrative style or tone, they said don't worry about it, just fill it out as best you can. So I did. They sent me back an edited version, asking me to redo it based on their edits. Their main concern was that I had not used the narrative style of the organization and it did not have the correct tone. I should've known at that point that we were not meant to be together.

I haven't had any online interviews that required me to recite the alphabet or do math on the spot. Still, there are a lot of issues that come along with virtual interviews that I need to address.

Chapter 24:
The Zoom Problem

Zoom, Teams, and Google Meet have become the norm, especially since the pandemic. Prior to the Internet, it was not an issue to take a screening phone call while sitting home on your couch in your underwear, unwashed for days while you loll around unemployed and sad. Nowadays, things turn quickly to a preliminary Zoom call which requires a lot more of the applicant.

I'm going to use Zoom here as a generic term for an online meeting. Sort of like Q-Tips are a name brand, but we all call all cotton swabs Q-Tips anyway. I have spent less time on Zoom than many of my friends. The pandemic brought a lot of workplaces into homes, as online meetings became mandatory and normal. I didn't experience that, since I worked mainly on my own, coaching track or baking sourdough bread. I did have some book clubs that met online during the pandemic. It was so weird at first. If only I'd known this would rapidly become the norm. I am not good at Zoom. Back then and even now, when I get on a Zoom I probably spend way too much time checking out what I look like, leaning my head a little left or a little right to look better. I check my makeup, my hair, and my outfit. I pray nobody notices that I'm doing any of that! It's a skill not to be distracted by your own appearance on Zoom. And yes,

I know there is a way to hide myself in my own view, but I don't. I always wonder if people see me as having grey hair or blonde hair, as the lighting can be iffy in the corner of my dining room that houses my "home office." Do I appear too old? Too young? Am I sitting weird, or did I put the laptop at that angle that shows all of my chins? Most of the time, I have managed to put on a nice shirt and some earrings to give the appearance that I'm a professional and not some-one sitting around in bike shorts and a ratty sweatshirt with three days of makeup still on my face. *I suddenly feel like I've said too much.* Well, this is a book about understand-ing, so hopefully those online interviewers will remember that the person at the other end put some work into looking like they do right now!

I was once in a Zoom meeting where one of the people, who held a higher position in the organization, was Zoom-ing from home. Their home was apparently very small and very messy, *and* they had on a bathrobe. I'm pretty sure they were reclined on their bed, too. I had a hard time not staring at them and their background the entire meeting. If that had been an interview, I as interviewer would seriously question their professionalism. A filter would be a good idea in this situation. Or even just claim the camera is not working. Technology is getting better and better for filters. It used to be that you would see people's homes, which I actually liked, as it sort of leveled the playing field a bit. I still use my house as my background most of the time because I designed it to be pretty and unassuming. ('Modern Farmhouse' if you are wondering.) I have seen people's messy kitchens as well as mansion views. I have made assumptions based on what I saw in some cases. Be sure to pay attention to what is going on behind you. We've all seen the videos of people's spous-es accidentally walking through a Zoom wearing no clothes. This is all manageable now! Control the setting.

On the same note, be aware of the noise in the environment. It's imperative to stay on mute most of the time, and be mindful of what is happening when the mute is off. I was recently in an interview where I was answering panel questions with five participants. I remember it was on a Monday afternoon because that's the day my yard crew comes by. On this particular day, they chose to walk across my deck three times using their very loud leaf blowers before I could do anything about it. My computer video was aimed outside onto the deck because for 99.9% of the week it is lovely, filled with lush, green trees, tons of birds, and squirrels. In this instance, it was embarrassing to share that yes, I pay someone to blow my leaves, and extremely irritating because it went on for a really long time and threw me off my thought process for the interview. I don't schedule Monday interviews anymore, even though the crew comes biweekly. Control the setting! As a dog owner, it is inevitable that the dog will act up during a meeting. For me, it's usually a squeaky toy that he feels needs to be shared or else he is barking at the squirrels who taunt him all day, every day. P L A N A H E A D !

CONTROL THE SETTING
Before you go live, do a full sweep. They can see everything

HOW YOU LOOK	HOW YOU SOUND	EVERYTHING ELSE
Lighting Light in front of you, not behind. Backlit = witness protection. Overhead only = instant villain.	**Pets** Relocate them. Lock the door. They will find the squeakiest toy and bark at nothing.	**Other People in the House** Let everyone know you are in a meeting. Someone will still walk by without pants.
Makeup Cameras are unkind. Wear more than you think you need. The screen takes 30% and keeps it.	**Landscapers** You cannot control them. You can only reschedule. There is no tech that filters a leaf blower.	**Your Background** Clean, neutral, intentional. They will read every book title and judge the plant.
Hair Check it again right before you join. It moves when you're not looking.	**Garbage Trucks** They know. They always know. They have been waiting for this day specifically.	**Your Phone** On silent. Face down. Your aunt will text during the most important question.
What You're Wearing Professional on top. Whatever on the bottom. Just don't stand up. Ever. For any reason.	**Workers & Construction** Warn them in advance. Bribe them if necessary. Silence has a price and it is worth paying.	**Notifications** Turn off every single one. Your computer will announce an email from your dentist at full volume.
Filter or Not A light touch is fine. Full beauty mode is a promise you can't keep in person. They will notice.	**Your Microphone** Test the day before. Not five minutes before. Laptop mics are designed by people who hate you.	**Join Early** Log in five minutes before. Sit in the waiting room. Breathe. Don't arrive exactly on time. That is late.
Camera Angle Eye level. Always eye level. Below the chin is a hostage video. Above is surveillance.	**Seasonal Distractions** Whether it is the mating call of the spring birds or the snowplows coming through in winter, close windows and doors, or sit away from the loudest part of the house.	**The To-Do Pile** Be careful leaving bills or letters where your eyes can wander. Your brain will try to focus on what needs to be done instead of who you are talking to now.

Chapter 25:
Trust Your Gut!

I have been in search of the perfect job for so long that I will often pretend that the crappy way I'm being treated is a one-off: *"If I can just get my foot in the door, it'll be great."* That isn't always the case. Often the way you're treated from the moment you make contact with the organization, either with an application or resume submission, is a reflection of how you'd be treated as an employee. Sometimes it takes a bit longer for the red flags to emerge, but if you're paying attention, they're often visible from the get-go. If you notice them, it's in your best interest to bring them to the forefront and address the issue right away. Trust me!

As a potential employee, take every opportunity to get information and ask questions. I've found with many jobs that the communication stream is one-way, leaving me in a lurch when I remember a question or want to find out the job status. A lot of companies like Indeed use middlemen to do the prescreening, and the interviewer's information is a highly guarded secret. This sucks. Sometimes jobs will be promised. You'll hear, "this will be a great place to work," and "you seem like you will fit right in," or "this will be your office," or "we will order your equipment tomorrow and start on Monday," only to be ghosted immediately afterward.

Automated responses to applications are normal. Of course, there are hundreds of applicants for a position and no real way to personalize a response. That makes sense. However, when the resumes have been screened and the candidates whittled down, I've found that it often remains difficult to find out what's going on. If I email into the void, I get a bounce-back, automated message telling me that they will reach out and contact me for further information if necessary or something like that. Often, on a job search page for different organizations, it's possible to see the status of the application. I have had jobs that show the status "resumes have been forwarded to the hiring party" for YEARS. No resolution, ever. It's silly, right? In this day and age, it makes sense to review the software and make sure it's completing the loop. It takes very little effort to let the candidate know what's going on. I could pull up governmentjobs.com right now and give a half dozen examples of a job that says my application is pending, which is not the case.

Another red flag is a dead reply to the initial application. This usually goes something like: "If you don't hear from us, assume we are not interested in interviewing you for the position."

What? If I don't hear by when? What happens to my application?

No information and permission to ghost!

What I find even more fascinating with these is that often, months and months later, when that application is long forgotten, a rejection email will arrive, saying: "Thank you for applying, your qualifications were reviewed and deemed not worthy of anything except a reminder of your lack of employability months after you spent all the time doing the application, cover letter and your 2,784,648th version of your resume." I may have added a couple of words there, but you get the gist. I have gotten sooooooooooooooooooo many email rejections for jobs I don't even remember applying for, long after someone else has been hired. Give me a break. You didn't want to hire me, so please just say so, in a timeframe where I can accept it and move forward with dignity.

Once the hunt gets going and I find that I'm a viable candidate, that's when the false promises flood in. I'm not sure why employers do this, unless it buys them time to find someone to hire who isn't me. I always imagine the hiring team sitting around looking at my application, the only one left in the pile, and saying things like, "there's nobody else left, what do we do now?"

"Hell hasn't frozen over, so we can't hire her. Let's just send this on to a different person and have them hold it for a month or two."

False promises most often show up in the initial Zoom interview. I'll ask a few questions, including an inquiry about when I'll hear back about more interviews, or if it's a final interview, when the decision will be made. It's amazing, but many teams say something like, "You're the last interview, we're meeting next week to make a decision," or "You're one of the first interviews, and we'll finish up in a couple weeks, then reach out for next steps."

By now, you know what happens. Crickets. No answer. No resolution. No next steps. No job. Rinse and repeat. When I finally get brave and reach out to see what's going on, my gut screaming at me that I already know the answer. I'm not surprised to hear that the position has been filled or that the posting has been canceled. It would be nice to hear that in a different way, that's all I'm saying!

There's one final red flag that I have had waved in front of my face a few times that I need to bring to your attention. Many times someone in an interview will complain to me about either the management, the organization itself, or the hiring process being broken. I'm not sure what the purpose of this could be. I take it as an omen that A. I will be offered a job which I will find to be horrible or B. They are asking for my help to break them out of there. I think what actually happens is it's a slip of the tongue on their part. I'm the kind of person that somehow brings on the TMI from people, whether hearing about someone's IBS at a party, or hearing about my accountant's messy divorce while I'm trying to file my taxes, or a cashier telling me their life story when all I want to do is buy my damn tampons and get out of there, this happens a lot. I'm a self-labeled empath so I absorb that shit like crazy which seems to bring on more of it! Employers, *I don't want this*. If you need some help with your internal organization troubles, please hire me as a consultant. I'm not doing this for free. Plus, I can't work here since you've already laid out just how troubled things are.

To recap: You know the feeling–that "uh oh" that pops in, whispering in your ear that something is not quite right? It gets squashed down, but it keeps showing up. Sadly, many of us ignore it and accept being treated as less than by a hiring party. After all, paying our bills becomes more important than trusting that we are in a good place. There's no reason to be unhappy or in an abusive work relationship. Strive to work somewhere that is a good fit, since we work for most of our lives.

Chapter 26:
The Internal Candidate Conundrum

I have applied for many jobs that aligned with my skills and interests, for organizations whose mission matched my own. In these frequent matches, I would send in my application, hear back fairly quickly, get through the screening interview and find myself in the group interview before much time has passed. This tends to be how it works when there are internal candidates for a position. Consider yourself warned if you are job hunting and the process is faster than usual: the interviewers are attentive, kind, and highly motivated to move through the process. In a lot of cases, there happens to be a candidate from their own organization who has already been interviewed and is going to be hired. Legally, they have to interview other candidates in order to show that they did their due diligence to bring their internal candidate on board. I really wish there was a way for job hunters to know at the onset that they are heading into a job interview where there is already a viable internal candidate. I feel like many times I have been used as a pawn in this game of hiring within.

You'd be amazed at all the information you can find online these days. LinkedIn provides the job history of different people within organizations, and social media can give a peek into who someone is. Back in the dark ages before the Internet existed, we didn't have the ability to do a lot of research on the company, nor did they have the ability to find out about us with a few clacks of the keyboard. I don't know if companies do this often, but as a job-hunter I definitely look up the place I'm applying to, see who works there and try to find out more about who they are as individuals, judgments I make based on social media posts. I realize that a lot of people lock down this information, but it's still part of my process when I'm heading to an interview.

While writing this book, I was interviewing with a couple of different organizations. I decided to look up the person who would be interviewing me on LinkedIn and Facebook to see what they were all about, since LinkedIn gave me a notification that she had also looked me up recently. Career-wise, we had a very similar background and had worked in similar fields. On Facebook, it was totally different information. That is the back pocket data I was hoping to talk to her about. I wondered if what I knew from Facebook would help or hinder me in this employment scenario.

What is the thing I knew? I discovered that she's Facebook friends with ten people I went to high school with in my very small hometown. Most of them are in the same friend group and I'm still friends with most of them, including my best friend who passed away 12 years ago and still has a Facebook profile. So there was something to talk about and I was hoping I would have the opportunity to at least figure out how our worlds have crossed. I was trying to come up with a way to bring it up casually in conversation, as my first phone interview there with someone else was very casual and we had a nice chat so assumed that because of the type of work it is, that the interview would lend itself to some casual chat as well.

Update 1: The interview ended up being panel-style on Zoom. A group interview is not a good time to call one person out to talk about why she knows ten people from my small-town high school. The interview went great so I hoped that I would progress to the in-person soon and maybe have an opportunity to have that conversation. I'm not a huge fan of panel interviews, especially on Zoom, but I muddled through. Everyone was very welcoming and kind.

Update 2: The morning after, bright and early, I got an email from HR saying:

"Thanks for your time interviewing. The hiring manager chose an internal candidate at this time to move forward with. I wanted to tell you quickly as I know you have been interviewing and looking for the best fit. We really appreciate your candidacy and good luck with your search."

I copied and pasted that directly from my email. My heart sank. I'd honestly felt a connection with this organization, and to find out I was only a pawn for their internal hire was very discouraging. I had to scream into a pillow for a few minutes lest I lash out and burn the bridge. The woman with whom I wanted to talk about our high school connections wasn't the hiring manager, but I contemplated reaching out to her to foster a relationship, lest another job pop up; there are a lot of pros for me to work at that particular place.

Oftentimes when I have gotten the dreaded "we hired an internal candidate" email I go through the grief and loss cycle, wondering what, if anything, I could have done to make me the best choice. I assume most often that the internal candidate gets priority treatment because they already know the nitty gritty of the organization. If I knew there were internal candidates before I accepted an interview, I would like to find out where the bar is set when they are comparing our skills. If they said they would only consider external candidates if they had something unique, like extra years of experience, more certifications or degrees or what-have-you, then I would feel okay about opting out of the interview if I didn't have those. As it is, to go through the time-consuming work that goes into interview prep, not to mention the often-expensive clothing upgrade, money and time to get there, etc, I would rather skip it.

Remaining professional, I replied with this:

"Aw damn, this is such a bummer. I am sad, of course. I hope that if any jobs within my realm of skills opens up you will not hesitate to reach out to me about it. I am such a fan of XXX's mission and I know it will be more and more important as we move forward through the upcoming months and years."

A few weeks after writing this, I saw another job open up and contacted HR who let me know they had already made an offer to yet another internal candidate. At least they didn't waste my time! I know you are wondering how this actually wraps up? As I alluded to in the beginning of this chapter, this was not the end. I added the woman on LinkedIn, and our paths did eventually cross.

Chapter 27:
Small World Syndrome

A few weeks after connecting on LinkedIn I saw that my new connection was looking for work. It made me more curious. Had I avoided working somewhere that was ultimately falling apart, narrowly avoiding unemployment and all that it brings with it? What was the truth behind that organization? I was determined to find out so I reached out asking her to meet up and told her about this book and my need for information. I wanted to supplement the previous chapter, but decided it needed a full one of its own. We agreed to meet for coffee as soon as we could, which with some life craziness, took a while. She then posted on LinkedIn that she had started a new job. Interestingly, my sister is on the board of her new organization, and I'd just attended an event there where my sister was the emcee and opening comedy act as well. I pointed this out to my new LinkedIn friend who asked if I'd been at that show. I said yes, and that I'd even written part of her act, was sitting front row center, and was the butt of jokes about many times during the stand up act. We thought that was pretty funny, *"what a small world!"* and finally set up our coffee meeting.

We finally met up and said our hellos. She was similar to me, late-50s, a hard-working mom with big goals to help raise money for nonprofits. Once we started talking, first about the comedy show and how we were both in the VIP lounge beforehand, I got into the high school questions that had been driving me insane. I told her where I went to high school, and that I grew up outside of town. *Where outside?* Addy. *Where outside of Addy?* Summit Valley. (Note: Summit Valley is a tiny, remote farming area, not an actual town, where I attended the two-room schoolhouse in 5th grade. Nobody has ever heard of it. By the way, it's neither a summit nor a valley.) She said, "I lived in Summit Valley!" My mouth dropped as we dialed in her story compared to mine and found that she lived near my grandfather's property, knew all of my childhood friends, and had indeed attended the same high school as me. She arrived there late, so we were only in school together for just over a year. I still didn't remember her until she said she played volleyball and was the varsity setter. Quickly, things started to clear up. I did remember a new girl being our setter my Junior year. We talked on and on about the people we knew, the stories we had, friends who had died, and were in shock about the insanity of how small the world was.

And then, if you can believe it, it got just a little smaller! When I got home, I dug out my high school yearbook from that year and found the volleyball team photo. There she was, and right behind her, leaning on her, was ME! THAT is a small world story!!!! (I'm top left, #15, she is right below me.) Why did they make all of us tall players bend over, though?

Despite not getting the job I interviewed for, I got this incredible story and hopefully a lifelong friend from it. Thank you, Susie! Who knows what projects we may work on in the future.

Chapter 28:
Va-Va-Voom!

One time, not long after I finished graduate school, I went for an interview at a health research company. I had the skills and experience needed, as it was a fairly entry-level position in a new organization. I was okay with that, as it had benefits and paid enough to live on. I may have been overqualified, but not egregiously so. I was happy to get an interview here. When I was finishing school, my mom had bought me some professional clothing to wear when I presented my thesis. I remember exactly what I wore to the interview, mainly because I thought I would be a little bit overdressed since I had on my new suit. This was the 1990s, so the suit had an over-sized long black jacket with structured shoulders (not 1980s shoulder pads), and a black skirt that came to just below my knees. I wore a brightly colored geometric sweater under the jacket. It was pretty, added some flair, coordinated with the suit and the high neck made it modest. I wore black tights, and a pair of low black pumps. Remember pumps? I had long curly hair and wore it down, parted on the side, with plain silver earrings. That was my interview uniform. I was 28 years old, so not super young but young enough.

On the day of the interview, I was nervous, as I always was. I went to the front desk and was asked to take a seat and wait to be called in. I remember the receptionist saying, "This will be a group interview." I had no idea what that meant. Maybe a few people interviewing me panel-style? Nope. What it meant is that there were four candidates for the same job, and we would all be in the room together. I'd never experienced this, and have not since then. It was very strange. Also in attendance: a gal about my age, wearing business casual (probably the one who was hired), a man who also had on a suit, who was a bit older than me, and an older woman wearing a frock/apron type thing, with weird pockets and some cat hair on it, with a turtleneck underneath it. I wondered if she had forgotten about the interview and had to rush out of feeding her cats to get there. I realize this sounds very judgmental, but it will make sense soon. What I did not do was leave the interview and immediately share this information with anyone!

We were asked questions by the interviewer, which I answered to the best of my ability. I don't really recall the actual interview after so many years, but the other candidates are burned into my head, probably because of what happened later. It is pretty unbelievable. At this time in history, there was no social media. It's strange that for a lot of my working years, we could not post on Facebook or look at Indeed. So what happened?

Back in the early days of the Internet, you could sign up for something called a *listserv*, which is kind of like joining a Group on Facebook now. You would be able to write something to a group of people with shared interests and an email and note would go out to all of them. One of my friends called me, someone for whom I'd worked in the past, and asked me if I was at a job interview that morning and if it had been a group interview. Of course, I had been and asked her why. She said there was a woman in one of her listserv groups saying that, at a group interview today, there was this one woman in there who was all "Va-Va-Voom" sexy. Apparently, she went on and on about just how sexy this woman was.

"She called you the Va-Va-Voom lady numerous times," my friend told me.

"Are you sure it was me?"

"Did you have on your suit?"

"Yeah..."

"And a sweater?"

"Yep."

"Was your hair down?"

"Uh-huh."

"Plus, the way she described you, it just sounded like you, because you are a sexy woman. I assume you were dressed well, not like you were going out to a club, right?"

I laughed. "Yeah, it's my new suit with a matching sweater and a pair of simple pumps. Not stilettos or anything. I didn't even wear very much makeup."

"Well," my friend concluded, "apparently this lady thought you were Va-Va-Voom!"

"Wait—is this the type of woman who would own a lot of cats?"

"Um, she's *totally* that type of person. Why?"

"Because there was a woman in the group who just looked like she crawled out of some sort of cat shelter to come to the interview. Looks like I'm her type."

We laughed and laughed, though deep down I was hoping I didn't actually come across as trying to leverage my sexuality to get hired. I don't think I did.

If you could see me then (or even now) you would know that I'm just tall, curvy, and yes, conventionally attractive. But I'm not an exhibitionist and I don't dress in any sort of risqué way. In fact, I have a lot of my own issues with my body and with clothing. I constantly struggle with what to wear because I want to look nice and avoid being perceived in the wrong way. That's probably why I end up buying new clothes and shoes before just about every in-person job interview.

I did not get that job. I'm guessing they went with the person who was more business casual, in the right age group, entry-level, and fresh out of college. Which is fine. It gave me a good story to tell, and I will never forget how it feels to walk around the world unaware of just how Va-Va-Voom I am.

You're Underdressed!

Chapter 29:
You're Underdressed*!

The title probably makes no sense to you, so let me explain. Back in college, a bunch of us were walking home from a club at 2 or 3 AM. There were lots of people out and about on the main drag next to campus. A police officer got on his bullhorn, hollering, "You're Under Arrest!" to someone (not from our group). We all thought they were saying "You're Underdressed!" and just about wet ourselves laughing about being arrested for being underdressed, probably in part due to the alcohol we'd imbibed earlier that night. Since then, we have always said that to each other when we for whatever reason talk about anything to do with the police. Hint, this story has to do with...drumroll...The Police Department. OK, now that you have a full explanation of the title, here is the story I know you've been waiting for!

So, as I've been hammering out words into this manuscript, I have also been going through quite the ordeal. As you know, I've been earnestly job hunting for a long while to find *the one*. My main grant contract was finished, with a successful submission and receipt of a huge grant for my client. Since my work there was done, it was onward and upward, time to find some work. Having recently had an accident, surgery, and many unexpected complications that resulted in long bed rest, I was desperate to do something, anything to make life more interesting.

As I sorted through jobs available on GovernmentJobs. com, I did my usual search for grant jobs. A few popped up so I applied for any that were within the parameters I had set for myself: not too far away, decent pay, good benefits, doing good things. Beyond that I hoped for remote work, even more money and other perks. I know that being a grant writer, I will never get hiring bonuses, but I can hope for a salary that will allow me to survive, save and eventually retire. One popped up that sounded perfect–it aligned with my experience, there was room to grow, it was very close to home, and I could even access it on the light rail. Plus the pay was pretty great. I applied, which on GovernmentJobs. com was a lot of work. On their site, I had to pick apart my resume and enter each and every item into its own section, so it took a while. I hate when it makes you do that when you have all of this wrapped up neatly in a newly edited resume. This was the tip of the iceberg, though. If only I'd appreciated how simple that part of the process was! If only I'd seen the many red flags!

I applied on July 2, 2024 for the job which, for shits and giggles, we will call "Grant Job with local Police Department." Instructions for applying were:

- Answer the Supplemental Questions when requested, which can be found on the Questions tab of the Job posting.
- We do not accept resumes and cover letters during the anonymous application screening stage, unless otherwise stated in the job description.
- Applicants advancing to the next stage may be required to provide a cover letter, resume, writing sample, and references.

Six weeks later, on August 20, 2024, I was contacted via message on their website and an email to let me know I'd been selected for an in-person interview. I scheduled this for the first available time which was September 11, 2024, *ten* weeks after my initial application.

I then got an email with some attachments, as an assignment to complete within a week. It was two announcement-type forms they wanted me to compile into another type of document, which they apparently use on a regular basis. Having not worked in public service before, I had to do some research to figure out what that format was and how it should look/read. Once I figured that out, I decided to give AI a try and had it assist me in creating the document. I still edited it but overall I leaned heavily on what at that point was very new technology. My thought process went something like this: *since I have not been getting called for interviews, I will try something new, since it is likely I will not advance through this.* I also thought that if I got the job, using AI might be part of it going forward so I should be familiar with it. Admittedly, I was a little flippant in asking ChatGPT to help me, but I was running out of motivation to job hunt and beginning to not care as much. Sort of like swiping right on everyone in the entire Tinder app but not wanting to go out on a date. After I submitted the document, they asked me to send a resume, which I redid for the 2,308,857th time and confirmed the interview date.

On September 11, 2024, 23 years after the terrorist attack on our country and almost 22 years after my last official full-time job ended, I walked into the Police Department to interview. Of course I had on some new shoes and a new shirt, plus I wore a black blazer. I daresay I looked quite different than I had 25 years ago when I wore a similar look to an interview (see Va-Va-Voom!). It was a panel interview with the person leading it in full police garb, guns and all. He would ultimately become my boss if I were hired. The first thing they asked me to do was to do a presentation based on the (AI) document that I'd submitted. Thankfully, they had a copy I could review! I did my best, hit all the high notes, and felt pretty good. I answered and asked a lot of questions. They told me that if I moved on, I would have to go through a background check, a very-very-very-very thorough background check, in order to work in the Police Department. Now, if I'd read the job announcement more closely, I might have noticed this in the fine print:

Due to the critical and high-security nature of police work, top candidates must pass a polygraph, drug test, and thorough background check.

During my (what I have since learned was called) Oral Board Interview, they mentioned that I would have to undergo a major background check if selected to continue through the hiring process. I tried not to act surprised, because really if you are working with sensitive information, a background check makes sense. The polygraph came as sort of a shock but I nodded and smiled and said my *goodbyes* and *thank yous* and *hope to hear from yous* with a positive tone in my voice. They did tell me as I was leaving that this will take a long time, three or four months even. I was taken aback.

It gets worse.

I was emailed soon after to come in for a more rigorous four-hour interview, to be held on October 3, 2024. Before I went in, I had to fill out and submit a packet with every single piece of information I could possibly know about myself. Name changes, addresses back to college (which for someone who liked to move every year, was a challenge), financial information and medical history (HIPAA be damned). This included every job, every employer, every person I ever met, every place I'd ever gone. It was crazy long and took me a few weeks to complete. I had to reach out to many friends and former colleagues to ask them to be one of ten personal references for me. I included as many friends as I could who worked in the public sector, with job titles I thought would show them that I'm a decent human who knows good people. Fire Chief, Municipal Court Judge, Doctor, etc. I hoped I had covered my bases so thoroughly that they would just go ahead and skip the rest of the background check.

The four-hour interview felt like someone was holding a spotlight on me until I gave up all of my secrets under oath. It was terrifying to sit in the room with that police officer. Many hours later, I left there having confessed to stealing a lip gloss in 7th grade, which is the worst crime I have ever committed. I figured I shouldn't hide anything. I also had to talk about any drug use, most of which involved smoking a joint in the last century–many decades ago! Still, I had to tell them about it lest the polygraph disagree in the future and knock me out of contention. At this point, I'd spent a full week gathering the reference information and trying to recreate my work history back to 1987, which was no easy feat for someone who had worked so many jobs. Tracking down contact information for people whose names I didn't even recall was tough. Somehow I managed to get it done.

During the interview, the officer said they were having a terrible time with hiring new people (he didn't say which people, whether non-officer or officers but I assumed it was all staff). Looking back after all the work I've done and the 6+ months that I put into this, I know why they have trouble! I asked him if I should stop looking for other work, if this interview meant there would be a job offer forthcoming. He said I should keep looking since there were "two or three others" also going through this. I question why I didn't just say "fuck this" and walk out. Who else has months to undergo this process, hoping that maybe a job offer will come in a few months? Apparently, two or three others, at least.

On October 4, 2024, I received a two-sentence email:

Your Background packet has been forwarded to Public Safety Testing (PST) who will conduct the remainder of your background investigation. Please be on the lookout for an email from Public Safety Testing for further instructions.

It wasn't even signed. Weird. It was now *three* months after I put in my application.

On October 8, I received an email from an outside agency that was to do the background check on me. They wanted the following items:

- Personal History Statement (this is a massive document, which I had to redo in a different format after the last interview)
- Driver's License – color copy
- Proof of Vehicle Insurance (insurance card)
- Social Security Card and Proof of U.S. Citizenship (Passport, Birth Certificate or Certificate of Citizenship or Naturalization)
- H.S. Diploma or G.E.D. Certificate and/or Transcripts (Obtaining my 1987 HS transcript was ridiculously hard)
- College or Technical School Diploma and Transcripts
- Military Discharge Documents (DD214 long form) and Military Performance Evaluations
- Civil Court Orders or Decrees (Divorce Decree, Bankruptcy, Child Custody, Protection or Restraining Orders, Liens, Civil Judgments, Garnishment Orders, etc.)
- Documentation of any Legal Name Change
- Professional Law Enforcement, Firefighting/EMS, and Dispatch Certifications (if you have previous experience)

- Basic training academy curriculum/syllabus hours, including training titles and the corresponding hours (if you have previous law enforcement/corrections experience)
- Complete law enforcement/corrections training record
- Employment performance evaluations and/or reviews (I don't know about you but I don't have these just sitting around, nor is it a thing I want to share with anyone!)

I got everything submitted after a few more hard-core hours of working on this, and was contacted on October 18 that I would have a phone interview on October 20 (a Sunday!?!) with a private investigator.

This private investigator went over the same information I'd gone over in the four-hour interview, word for word, plus a bunch more questions I'd already answered on my forms, to determine that I was not lying. He went through each and every reference –I'd sent 10–and we discussed my relationship with each and how we met and all that jazz. He also went through my family and work relationships, again confirming that I was not lying about anything. He then said he would be contacting the references in the next few weeks and would talk to me once he finished. A few days later, people started getting phone calls from him, each time reaching out to me to tell me about their conversations. Eventually the calls stopped and he called me to say he had finished up and was going to write his report up and submit it back to the police department for next steps. This was early November.

CRICKETS

CRICKETS

In January 2025, I realized six months had gone by since I applied. Since originally applying for the job: I went on a cruise, my boyfriend moved in, my kid moved to Chicago for college, he came home for Thanksgiving, both kids flew home for Christmas, we got a puppy, I finished physical therapy, I got a job, lost a job, worked at the costume shop, lost another job, there was an election, and I went on a couple of trips. What I hadn't done was hear the outcome of the police department's hiring decision.

Did I even still want the job? Earlier in the process I was unsure, but decided to continue just to see if I could pass the background check. At this point I was pretty disgusted with the entire process. I didn't have a job offer. In fact, I didn't even know exactly what the expectations of the job would be. Remote? In person? Where is the office? What is my desk like? Is it a cubicle or a cool downtown office? At that point, they knew every single thing about my life, my past, my friends and family, and I knew nothing. It was rude and I was pretty sure that wasn't the place I wanted to be. But. I still didn't have a job. So, what was a girl to do?

I saw three ways that I could figure this out. The first way would be to contact them and ask. But who wants to do that? It had been seven months by this point. I wasn't in the mood to talk directly to them unless it was listening to a job offer. The second way would be to move on and ignore it until the end of time, accepting that I'd been ghosted after the most intensive, grueling job interview experience ever. Since I was in the midst of writing this book, I knew my readers would want to know what happened so I didn't just lay back and accept the ghosting. The third way, what any resourceful Gen-Xer would do, was to do some investigation. It wasn't hard. I entered the job description into LinkedIn, immediately being directed to a post from a woman saying "I'm happy to announce I am starting my new position as [local police] Grant Writer."

Well, there it was. They had hired someone, and she had started at the end of January. I went and looked on GovernmentJobs.com just to make sure I hadn't missed a message that I wasn't hired, and there was my application, still saying I was scheduled for the Oral Board review (back in September).

I was angry. Angry at them, but also angry at myself. In a process riddled with red flags, I felt shame that I had ignored them all. It took some honest self-talk before I realized that the actual job was something I would have been very good at, and that I didn't need to feel shame about how it ended. This one was not my fault. I went ahead and shared my experience with my ten references, all of whom were mortified to hear that it had ended so badly.

Then, I wrote a *strongly worded email** expressing my outrage at the sheer disrespect of it all. Instead of sending it and immediately regretting it, I let it sit for a while. But ultimately, my need for closure was too strong. I edited it and sent it, adding and removing CCs and BCCs until it went to just a couple of people in the police department and the HR department.

Then, as you would expect, C R I C K E T S .

But wait, then something happened!

Five days after sending my email, eight months after submitting my initial application, I got a call from the Police Chief. He was very apologetic, saying he was completely at fault for the lack of communication. He told me he was initially going to email me but decided against it because I deserved to hear his apology in person. He praised my email, as well as my professionalism regarding the bungling of the job recruitment. I joked, asking if he had any jobs open for people who were good at writing strongly worded emails. He surprised me by telling me about a position that was about to open up in a few weeks. "If you're interested," he encouraged, "let me know."

In case you're wondering, which I know you are, I didn't get my hopes up. Still, it felt great to hear that it wasn't me, it was them! I will be sure to pay attention to those red flags from here on out. Trusting that instinct is so important!

And no, I did not apply for any other jobs at the Local Police Department.

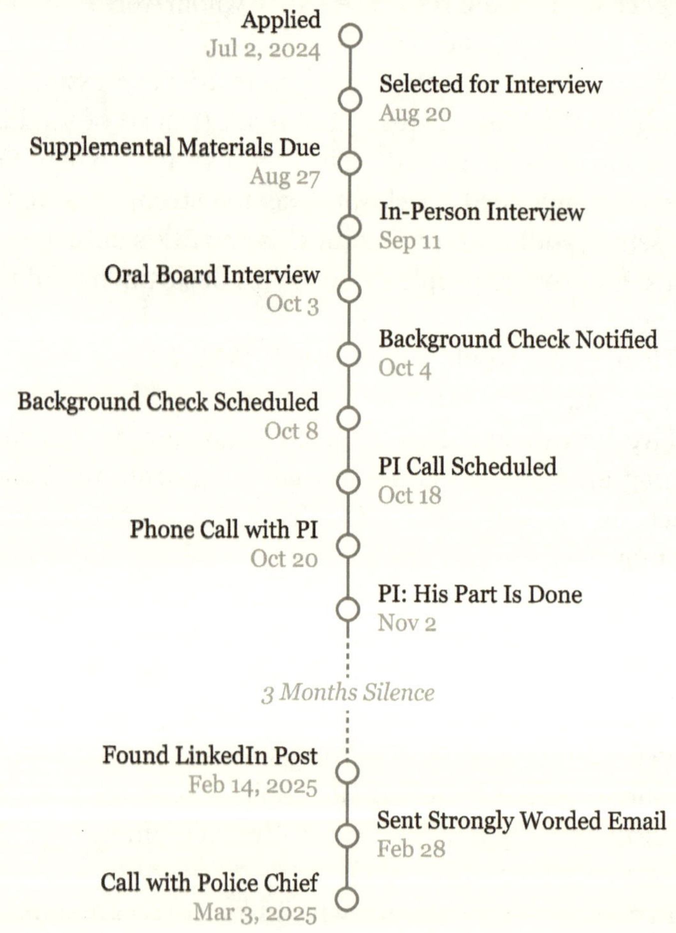

*I know you were wondering what my email said. Here it is for your reading pleasure:

To Whom It May Concern:

I am writing to formally express my dissatisfaction with the hiring process for the Police Grant Administrator at ▮▮▮▮▮▮▮ Police Department, specifically regarding the lack of communication and my experience as a qualified candidate.

After six months of undergoing a comprehensive background check as well as multiple interviews, I was shocked to learn via searching for the position on LinkedIn that I was not selected. At no point during this process did I receive any direct communication from your department regarding the status of my application or of a final decision. The last I heard was a phone call from the PST Investigator ▮▮▮▮▮▮▮ at the beginning of November letting me know that his investigation was complete and that he was forwarding the results to ▮▮▮. Having been told at both in-person interviews that the process was going to be months-long, I didn't worry too much since it was the holidays, and mistakenly assumed I would soon find out the status. Instead, my curiosity got the best of me and in mid-January, I searched for the results myself. The Government Jobs website, where I initially found the posting, still, in Mid-March(!) indicates that I am in the interview process. I have waited to send this in hopes that some final letter or other communication to allow for closure was forthcoming, however, I realize that is not the case so am sending this now.

This lack of transparency and follow through is both frustrating and highly unprofessional. Given the significant time and resources that applicants invest into your hiring process, basic courtesy would dictate that applicants are notified of decisions in a timely and direct manner. Instead, I was left to learn the outcome through a third-party source, which I find bitterly disappointing.

I would appreciate an explanation as to why such a crucial element of your hiring process, specifically, clear communication with applicants, was neglected. It is essential that organizations like the ▮▮▮▮▮▮ Police Department uphold professional standards and respect applicants' time and efforts throughout the hiring process. Being under such scrutiny during the aforementioned background check was both excessively time consuming and nerve wracking. To hear nothing back after that process was insulting on many levels. I am not seeking a bullet-point list of why I was not selected for this job. Instead, I would like to make sure that going forward, other candidates are treated with professionalism and respect for their time and energy during this grueling process.

I look forward to your response and hope that my feedback will be taken seriously.

Section Seven

Why Not Me?

Chapter 30:
Who Gets The Last Word?

Gather around, boys and girls, and let me tell you a tale about what used to happen after a job interview. We would either get a phone call to offer us a job, or we would receive a letter with an explanation of why we did not get the job. The explanations were rote and repetitive, awfully similar to the mass rejection emails of today. There has not been a great deal of change there. One thing that was often done back then, though, was a thank-you card. I would carefully and thoughtfully handwrite a clever note to whoever interviewed me, thanking them for their time and sharing my excitement in becoming their next great employee, and send it through the mail.

I don't know about you, but I have a ton of boxes of random crap, mostly paperwork, in my garage. Despite ongoing purging and constant moves, it still exists. It seems like every time I open up a box to purge, I find another pack of thank-you cards that were once used to send to interviewers. I was an expert thanker. I think this is a lost skill, as my kids' generation seems to struggle to write anything on paper, much less on an actual card—and god forbid they have to figure out how to write an address and learn where a stamp goes! The point is, I sent a lot of thank-you cards. I can't say for sure whether it tipped the scales toward employment or not, but I did it anyway.

As technology came on board and email communication became the norm, I would pivot and send a thank-you email *if* I had the interviewer's contact information. I understand the reasons why we are often not given direct email or phone numbers to people in a company, as the information could be misused (not by me). Still, I always try to let someone know I appreciate their time and am interested in the job, or at least another interview. These days, through the apps, I have had to rely on the middleman passing my message along to the hiring party. I can't guarantee this happens, but I feel better knowing I put in the effort and completed my end of the deal.

It seems like with job hunting apps, there is a potential for each open position to get hundreds of applicants and for them to screen a high percentage of them before whittling it down to Zoom interviews. Still, having been in a lot of zoom interviews, it seems like there are still a dozen applications for each interview. Perhaps it's the field I'm in, but in speaking with others, it seems commonplace to have a lot of competition for every job. I can't imagine being the person who receives thank yous for any interviews done in this hectic situation. That would be a lot. It would be great to get closure at the end of the interview. Something to the effect of, "while we appreciate some candidates would like to send us follow up emails, we don't have the bandwidth to read through them. Please wait for us to reach out in the next two weeks with further steps." It really is up to the hiring organization to set the standard for this. And maybe, just maybe, be happy when they receive a rare handwritten thank-you note through the mail.

In one interview, decades ago, there were seven people on the interview panel. In hindsight, I probably overdid it, writing each person a thank-you card which highlighted something they had talked about during the interview. Perhaps I appeared too overeager, or maybe they thought I was fake. I'll never know. I still remember all the notes I jotted down in my notebook after the interview, sitting in my car in the parking garage, my heart full of hope, then carefully writing each card in my perfect penmanship and sending them off. Penmanship? I know. Who writes anything now? I feel like some of these soft skills would be excellent in the workplace. I think they are possibly seen as antiquated and even annoying at this point. Still, I do write thank yous when I can.

Whether or not thank you cards make a difference in hiring, there is, more often than not, a rejection coming. While I appreciate having closure, I don't like a great interview ending in a letter that talks about how much they loved me but are not ultimately offering me a position. Despite best intentions and protocol, interviews are always a place where anything can happen.

Chapter 31:
Baby Face

I save rejection letters the way other people save love letters. They're kept in a manilla folder of their own, carefully arranged by date of rejection. Each one tells a story.

When I was 22 or 23 years old, I was just getting into the swing of applying for jobs. I'd been working survival jobs and one "real job" but hadn't had to put myself out there yet. Perusing the classified ads in the newspaper, I would circle many job announcements, in a variety of fields. I typed cover letter after cover letter on expensive paper reserved solely for job hunting. It was akin to spraying perfume on a love letter. *This employer will see how desirable I am, they will not forget me!*

I always felt like an adult, even as a child. I translated my precocious adulting ability into confidence when applying for and interviewing for jobs. I think about this now as I'm on the flip side, experiencing ageism in hiring. But I'll get into that in a later chapter.

I'm sure that deep in my files resides a rejection letter letting me know that as a 23-year-old recent college graduate, they "appreciate my enthusiasm" but feel I "need a bit more experience" before trying to become the CEO or Director of Staff. I honestly felt in my heart that I had what it took for those types of positions. I had not burned out yet and felt I had so much to give.

Some of my early "jobs" required a lot of me. I was a caregiver for years, dealing with the intricacies of activities of daily living as well as the bureaucracy of healthcare, transportation, and education systems. Coupled with this, I was also helping my dad navigate similar systems as he worked towards returning to independent life. I didn't have a grasp on the full intricacies of running an organization, despite my inner voice and overly confident ego thinking I did.

In my 20's, I wanted to share how my unique situation created the most responsible human on earth. I thought putting such personal stuff in a letter was in bad taste, so I did not share it. Now, as a 57-year-old with decades of life and work experience, I hint at personal stories, leaving employers wanting to know more. I try to make them want to see me after receiving my letter, so to speak.

Having moved to new schools many times as a child, I'd become very good at connecting with people instantly. I carried this into my adulthood. My confidence in establishing rapport usually led directly to my fantasy about what a successful career would look like. I will admit to having spent a great deal of time thinking about what clothing I would wear for work, what briefcase I would carry, and what glasses would make me seem smart. What I neglected to do was to take a good look at how I was presenting myself on paper to these companies.

In reality, I didn't have a lot of money and when I did get the rare interview, I'm sure I looked like a pauper, a kid wearing their mom's shoes and pearls. I couldn't hide my dyed black goth hair and dark circles from partying all weekend and being professional all week. I lived in a constant state of desiring to be one thing while actually being something quite different. It makes me cringe to think of the interviews I went into, taking myself so seriously, and having everyone wonder what the heck this awkward, pasty, chubby, goofy kid was doing in their boardroom.

Chapter 32:
Older Than Them Thar Hills!

My formerly Va-Va-Voom body has had children, been through a pandemic, been a triathlete, gotten injured, had surgery–it has gone through marriage, divorce, death of friends, family and pets, remodeling, house selling and every other kind of stressor. This is how I have become so finely aged. My hair is not brown any longer, my skin has wrinkles, my menopausal body is real, and I move more slowly and hold myself differently than I used to. Still, compared to my peers of the same age, I do okay. I think people still perceive me as being younger than I am, based on how often cashiers at grocery stores call me sweetie, or how surprised people are when I mention my age. When I'm job hunting, though, the gray hair and tell-tale resume have definitely kept me from being hired in a few places.

Writing a resume for a job has changed over the years. It used to be that you would list your education, when you graduated, where and what degree(s) etc. Then you would go into your job history, where and when, and on to volunteer work or what-have-you. As the years have gone by, there has been a shift and it isn't recommended to put years on some of the topics. I know that if I list that I graduated college in 1991 and 1998, a resume reviewer born in 2001 will likely move mine lower in the pile. Once I started taking the year of graduation off my resume, I got more calls for interviews.

The same goes for job history. If someone sees my 35+ years of work history, and that person is only 30 years old, I can understand how that might feel intimidating. I know that's how I felt when I was in my 20s. One time, I hired an employee much older than me who turned out to be an exceptional team member, and from then on, I knew that it doesn't matter if they have grey hair and have done a lot of things, if they are a dedicated employee and an excellent person in general.

When I was young, in my 20s and early 30s, I generally worked with people of similar age due to where I was in my career and the field I was in. It was common for my colleagues to step away to get married and soon after go on maternity leave. It was just how it was, and still is. The cycle of life goes on. Some would return to work, others would not. Prior to having kids, I didn't understand how hard it was to make that decision. I do know that my experience of being discriminated against for getting pregnant shed light on how much a female has to endure as she moves up the career ladder, especially if she is of childbearing age. It is illegal to ask details of marriage or planned pregnancies during the interview, so assumptions do happen. The middle years of life, one in which kids get sick or there are school holidays and summer vacations to manage, are equally stressful for the employee as well as for the employer who may be taking a risk by hiring someone who may not be as committed to their work as someone without outside responsibilities. I wonder why someone who has already gone through those milestones is not treated as the most valuable resource to a company looking for a dedicated employee.

I had an interview a few months ago for a senior-level position where I was markedly older than the three women interviewing me. They were in equal or higher roles within the organization. I would have reported to someone who was probably around 35. I immediately felt old when I sat down with them. I'd already had a phone interview and a Zoom interview prior to this final round. On the video call, I'm not sure if I appear grey-haired or blonde. But in person, I definitely have grey hair. The job required maybe a dozen things to be a strong candidate. I had every single item, and then some, when all of the years of experience were added up. I knew I would be getting a job offer and was very keen on the opportunity. I asked if they had admin staff to support this position and they said they were hiring a junior-level staff specifically for that. The one question they asked that I was not prepared for was, "What is your 15-year plan?" First of all, who has a 15-year plan? I have a one-year and a five-year, but beyond that it's a crapshoot! We left after meeting a lot of people in the building who would be my colleagues. They said I would hear soon and that the next steps were a job offer and onboarding. To me, it felt good.

Ping The email rang to remind me to look at my new messages. There it was. The offer!

Nope. Instead, it was, "We really enjoyed meeting you and think that you have a ton of experience that would be great for our organization. However, we are going a different direction and will continue to recruit other candidates. You might want to consider applying for the Junior-level position in the meantime."

Holy fucking hell. I cannot say with certainty that it was my age, but looking at every other factor and considering it was the third interview, I cannot come up with anything else. I do realize they may not have felt the same vibe that I did, but this is my book. The insulting part was being told to apply for the entry-level position that would support the role I'd just interviewed for. I knew from experience what could/would happen. My confidence and capability would lend me to take on more and more work but I would get paid and treated as the entry-level person. Again, if I were new in the field, I might try that, but I had managed multiple projects and had tons of experience doing what they wanted me to do. I ghosted them and didn't reply. That bridge can smolder for a while.

Months later, I see they are still advertising for the senior-level position. I get an email about it from various job-hunting websites regularly. I also got three emails from that same organization to please come and attend an open-hire day for all of their open positions, including that one. Needless to say, I skipped it.

A grey-haired lady such as myself would bring passion, available time both physically and mentally, and experience and connections that would enhance everything else that I have to offer. I think that people who are hiring need to step back and rethink discriminating against older hires. Older now means 35 and up in many fields. Us oldies have been through the school of hard knocks as well as everything else. You would not be bad off to give it a try. I promise. Ask us in interviews what our 5-year plan is, not our 15-year plan. I'll bet that answer would surprise you when we talk about elevating your organization to become more successful. In 15 years I want to be chilling on a beach somewhere, but in 5 years I will be celebrating the outcome of a hell of a lot of hard work.

You might think that I get passed over not for how old I am, but for having so much life experience. When someone interviews for a job and is obviously overqualified, is that a good or bad thing? In some job markets, it's a buyer's market, so the company can get someone with a lot of skills for less pay. Other times, overqualified candidates are appealing to hire for the litany of skills they have. However, there is a dark side. It doesn't take long for them to realize that they are unsatisfied and lose their morale, sense of faith in the company and become an employee who is out looking for a new job already.

Chapter 33:
Overqualified

There is always a learning curve when starting a new job. In addition, most job postings don't have a way to actually get to the meat of what the job really is. Things change, and when new people come on board, there is a natural shift in the way work is done. Humans are not copy/pastable. What happens, then, when an applicant applies for a job where they have every qualification listed? Do they automatically get an interview and job offer since they already know everything and that would require less onboarding and training on the part of the hiring party? Or, do they accept a job, quickly come up to pace and get bored? What about the hiring team? Do they really want to bring someone in who already knows everything to do with the position? In the case of a doctor, this is great, we want this! In a lot of other positions, it's better to have a grey area between what is already known and everything that is needed to master the job. It allows for personal growth through challenge and gives the employee an elevated self-esteem to achieve their mastery in doing the job their way, not just being a cog.

Part of the onus is on the job hunter. As someone who is going through job postings and applying to a variety of openings, it is important to be able to identify, at least a best guess, what level the position is compared to your skills and experience. I have made this mistake more times than I can count. In my experience, if a high school degree is the mandatory education, I have learned that this type of job isn't in the cards for me. For one, I won't generally get an interview (because, yes, I have tried), and second, I have done an excessive amount of entry-level type work in my career and I understand that I will not be satisfied in that job. The more desperate I have been in job hunting, the more I tell myself that I can do an entry-level job "for a while" and be okay. *Seeker, know thyself.*

There's nothing wrong with entry-level jobs and, in fact, some of the best days at work in my career have been doing admin work or pulling weeds. Since those days, I've gathered experience and education, piling it all on in order to be able to play a role in the success of a project, department, or agency. At my advanced age, I have a hard time seeing myself as the happy front-desk girl in a faculty office, smiling and helpful to all. I've seen things! I need to be able to dig into policy, put pen to paper, and create. *Know thyself.*

Some people are excellent and capable at any type of work, and I do love and appreciate that. Even jobs that are useful and seem fun are things I would be terrible at. Cashier, not me. I have no patience with myself, with lines, with being in a hurry. When I do seasonal (Halloween) work at the local costume shop, they have me work directly with customers, creating their unique looks, not using the cash register as it's just not my jam.

What if a candidate appears who the employer knows is overqualified, but they want to interview them anyway? "Just in case" it is a match, when they know that it probably is not. I think this stems from people's past experience of hiring a stellar person who, despite being overqualified, took the job and excelled at it without complaint. The worse the job market is, the easier it is to experience this, or to be that person. Sometimes, there's a hope that a position where they are better qualified will open up, so they had better get them hooked now lest they lose them to a competitor. But what if that upward movement through the organization doesn't happen, the employee is dissatisfied, and quits? Or, they are asked to work harder and harder, surpassing their supervisor's responsibility, but not credited for that work? That can get really complicated.

In my case, I was a couple of years out of grad school and running my own business doing consulting. The job market was changing as the dotcom era was about to crash and my clients were disappearing. I knew I needed a steadier job. I applied and interviewed for a ton, but none provided offers. It was discouraging and I was growing more and more desperate as I needed to pay bills and get insurance. I applied for a fairly entry-level job that needed some medical experience, which I had. I was hired part-time after a group interview filled with smiling, happy staff members who could not wait to tell me how much they loved working on this team. It didn't pay well but had benefits and the promise of career longevity and growth. I took the job. On day one, my gut said, RUN, QUIT, LEAVE! I ignored it, despite a bushel of red flags showing up day after day. It didn't take long to master the work and get bored. At the same time, the team hated the boss, the newly-merged company, and above all, they hated outsiders such as myself.

I want to emphasize that I in no way think I was better than any of the employees. The work itself just was not what I felt I was meant to do in my lifelong quest to change the world. Entering data and reviewing charts was so tedious. They knew when they hired me that I had a Master's degree and a lot of experience. In hindsight, the smiles around the conference table at the interview were the fakest I have ever seen. I still remember that day and have often compared and contrasted it against what the job really was. I feel like the organization was desperate to have someone come in with tough skin who was a sucker for abuse and that happened to be me at that moment. If they had been honest about what the job actually entailed, I think I would have passed and let me tell you, a lot of things in my life would be different today!

So how do we stop the insanity that is the time and money waste of an overqualified candidate? For starters, posting an accurate representation of what the job expectations are should be first and foremost. The job description needs to be transparent and authentic! Going on about small things like the ability to sort pencils into levels of sharpness is probably too intricate, so please be aware if the description has been doctored to make it seem more difficult than it is. If it is entry-level, it should say entry-level. If the job requires a certain level of education or certifications, be sure that the actual job responsibilities and pay reflects that. Once resumes are reviewed, be sure to highlight those that are definitely overqualified, even though you really think you would like to hire someone so competent. It isn't going to end well! If someone is in the gray area, where perhaps you think they may be overqualified, come up with a couple of screening questions to ask during a phone interview that can immediately signal that this person is not right for the job, and then tell them why! Don't just go dark and ghost them. A candidate who is hearing they are overqualified can definitely utilize that information when looking at other positions in the company or pivot and search differently.

As a job seeker, it would be most helpful to be able to ask some questions to accurately determine whether the depth and breadth of this job is what you are seeking. A short phone interview that welcomes those questions, or email correspondence at the very least, will make a big difference.

It isn't necessary to apply for every single job on the internet (ask me how I know). Many of them are just not right. It is like dating-you don't have to say yes to every date–you can screen out most of them and then keep asking questions to determine whether there is a match. Setting up a dozen interviews sounds impressive, but if most of them are not the right type of job, it is a huge waste of not only your time and energy but the very important emotional resources that keep you moving forward and support that confidence in your job search that is so crucial.

There is a lot of similarity between being overqualified and underqualified. There is that tasty grey area in job hunting that provides the perfect complement between having enough experience and/or education to do the job and enough of the unknown to learn more and excel at it, thus remaining happy at work, which is the ultimate career goal!

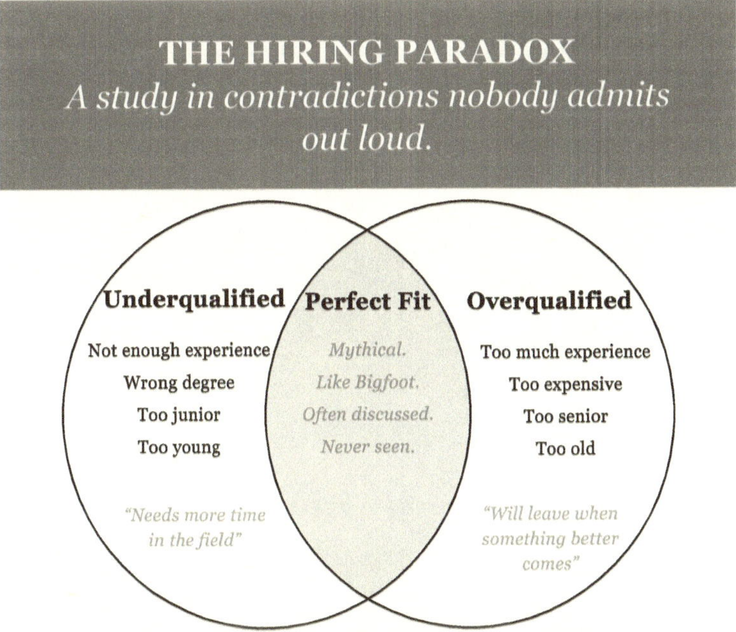

Chapter 34:
Underqualified

Determining if you, as the candidate for an open job, are underqualified can be tricky. Confidence can mask detriments.

Of course, if the position requires a PhD or MD, or a degree in nursing or certain licenses or certifications, I know that I'm not qualified, so I won't apply for it. Once in a while, I let my sixth sense take over and convince me that nobody would do better at that job and they will know that once they meet me. If they only *suggest* that those degrees or certifications are necessary, I might go ahead and submit my resume because of my vast experience working in healthcare and with whatever population they're serving. There are also jobs like CEO and Director, where perhaps I have not managed a $10 million budget nor have I had 500 employees beneath me. I probably wouldn't apply for those, knowing I have a snowball's chance in hell of getting any sort of follow-up. Even if the job sounds interesting, I think I would probably consider it and run it through the scenarios outlined at the beginning of the book, in Online Dating vs Applying for a Job.

There are times, too many to count, when it appears the job description was written by a past employee who was trying to get a raise because of how much they did, with every single task itemized. "Be able to use a staple remover."

"Have the ability to lift 40 pounds so you can change the office water bottles." The list of tasks, skills, errands, and every little thing is as long as the unemployment line. Meanwhile, the actual job requires an entirely separate skill set, which you will have to discern through a combination of observation, interrogation, improvisation, and possibly black magic. I wish that anyone posting a job would include a description of the ideal candidate. Some of us are very, very good at staple removal and lifting water bottles, but may not be so great at managing a branch of a bank or driving a light rail train.

With my non-traditional background, I can easily convince myself that I qualify for every job that tickles my fancy. Here are some of the jobs I have recently applied for (outcomes in parenthesis), bolstered by my background and long list of past job titles. Here's hoping my consistent rejection makes you all feel better about your own employment journey. Never give up hope; that perfect fit may be right around the corner.

- Grants to Organizations Program Coordinator (not selected, ghosted)
- Quality Assurance Training Program Manager (not selected, ghosted)
- Roads to Community Living Policy Program Manager (ghosted)
- Federal Grants Coordinator (phone) (Excellent interview, ghosted)
- Police Grant Administrator* (see chapter 29 about the world's longest interview process)
- Transportation Grant Administrator (ghosted)
- Union Grant Writer (not selected, ghosted)
- Healthcare Compliance and Privacy Specialist (internal referral, rejected the next day)

- Surgical Clinic Supervisor (internal referral, rejected within an hour)
- Bereavement Clinician-Hospice Home Care (not selected, ghosted)
- Vocational Rehab Counselor (not selected, ghosted)
- Grants Manager-multiple organizations (no job offers, a variety of rejection scenarios)
- Grants Manager-Arts Corp (Zoom, in person, strange group interview, not selected)
- Development Manager (not selected, ghosted)
- Director of Education, Sports Management Nonprofit (not selected after extensive group interview)
- Food Bank Grant Writer (multiple excellent interviews, lost to internal candidate)
- Parks Department Grant Manager (internal referral, not selected to interview)
- Lead Grants Manager, Boys and Girls Club (two interviews, ghosted, still don't know)
- Advancement Writer (Internal referral, Zoom interview, ghosted)
- Senior Grant Writer (3 interviews, not selected but told I could apply for their entry-level position)
- Grant Writer-Repertory Orchestra (multiple interviews with board members, not selected)

Whew! That is a shit ton of rejection. Is shit ton the official measuring weight of rejection? Let's go with yes. I really hope that made you feel better because it made me feel like crap!

How the heck do I make sense of all these mixed messages? I wish I could get some actionable feedback instead of "job closed/position filled," or worse, crickets, as it seems next to impossible to get my foot into any door without knowing what went sideways.

The way I deal with it is to tell myself, "it's their loss" because that's how I dealt with rejection when dating as a teenager and because my mom always said that to me. And because I really do feel like it's their loss. Maybe, as I have written in other chapters, I wasn't perfectly qualified for those jobs, but I know that my enthusiasm and willingness to do hard work would bring renewed energy to their organization. Nobody works harder than someone who has managed to keep their own business afloat for the last decade.

The alternative is to assume I must be lacking in basic skills that they had listed on the job postings. But this is a hard sell, since I never apply for anything requiring any licensing, education or certification that I don't already have. I'm pretty good at in-person interviews and am often (not always) offered a job after meeting in real life. The trick is getting to that stage, and it seems to be getting trickier.

I fully understand that hiring someone incompetent or vastly unqualified for a job can sink the ship. I've had near-sinkings in the past. Still, there's a desirable gray area where the candidate can fire up a department, work hard, and really make a difference. Reaching toward job mastery can boost the ego and keep an employee happily employed and make a huge difference in a department.

The solution? Screening questions. There they are again. This will save a lot of time and energy in the long run.

1. Does the job description list requirements you don't have?

2. Are they asking for a degree you don't hold?

3. Does the role require managing people and you've never managed anyone?

4. Is there a required certification or license you would need to get first?

5. Do you understand maybe half of the job description?

6. Have you googled more than three things in the job posting just to know what they mean?

7. Does every other applicant likely have more direct experience than you?

8. Are they asking for 5+ years of experience and you have one, or none?

9. Is the salary range three times what you have ever made, or ever thought you were worth?

AND FINALLY...

10. Do you apply anyway because the title sounded impressive?

11. Is your plan to learn on the job for literally every requirement listed?

12. Did you read "fast-paced environment" as a challenge rather than a warning?

Chapter 35:
Ghosted

I have been ghosted so many times that I could actually become a Ghostbuster (™). I don't think I'm alone in this. Whether it's a date who didn't text back, a customer service person who was going to call right back and never did, or a job where you felt a connection and then disappeared from the face of the earth, being left hanging is the worst. I daresay it is the part of job hunting that I loathe the most. I hate a lot of the aspects of this process, so that is saying a lot!

The unique thing about getting ghosted during job hunting is that it can happen at any time in the process, and for no apparent reason. It's become hard to get excited about a job prospect when there's an underlying suspicion that they will never talk with you again, if at all.

Resume-gathering bots muddy up the waters, and recruitment apps can stumble around professionalism and leave applicants in the dark. Again, it's a combination of respect and authenticity in the hiring process that can bust this rampant ghosting.

Over the years, I've been ghosted hundreds of times, and each time I'm as shocked as I was the first time it happened. I was raised to be kind and respectful to everyone I encountered, and part of that is being accountable for follow-through. If it is early in the cycle, I've learned to let it go. I guess with age comes wisdom. But just like in dating, the longer and more involved the relationship, the more it stings when they suddenly vaporize. No text after a first date? Whatever, *it's their loss*. Total radio silence after a third date during which they wondered aloud what our kids would look like? *Not okay.*

It's a close race on which I dislike more: ghosting or robo-reply, but I think that ghosting ekes out the win. I've had a lot of phone screening interviews. Many times, I make it to the next interview phase, but there are times when this doesn't happen. There have been plenty where I had a good rapport with the interviewer, talked about next steps, and then waited and waited and waited, never to hear anything ever again. No generic email that says the job has been filled. Just a big old crevasse in communication. This drives my inner professional insane and bruises my ego at the same time.

Sometimes the process moves along well, and there's an actual interview. These days, it seems like many organizations are opting for a Zoom interview before an in-person meeting, which I can't stand, but tolerate. Recently, I applied for a job that was a little funky looking on paper, but it had some appealing aspects, so I took a shot. Lo and behold, I got a Zoom interview. The panel-type, which I detest, but still, it was a foot in the door. The interview went well, and the group was really nice. I saw them as people I could actually work with. They asked about my puppy and shared their pets on screen with me since they were all working from home. The job itself was actually different than what was posted, and aligned almost exactly with a job I had succeeded at in the past. The team appeared excited that I grasped what this job entailed. I asked them intelligent questions at the end and finally asked what the next steps were. They said they had one or two more interviews the next day, and I would hear back within the week. To this day, I still haven't heard back.

In another recent interview, I learned more about the position and realized pretty early on I didn't have the qualifications they needed, although I was willing to learn. As we continued through the Zoom group panel questions (again, ugh) I knew it wasn't a good fit. Still, it was an organization I liked and respected, so I held out hope that if I got into a job there, I would eventually find my way to the right spot. Halfway through the interview I was given a chance to speak freely, and I did say, "I realize I'm not exactly qualified for this job, but I have been able to step into a job and achieve success many times throughout my career. However, I will understand if you just want to stop talking to me right now." They all laughed and said they were really enjoying our conversation and wanted to finish the interview. So, with that, we all had our say, and ended the interview with more friendly banter. Again, they let me know they were finishing up interviews and would be in touch very soon. Guess what? Another company added to my list of places I will never think of kindly again. Never a word.

I have used job hunting apps a lot recently. Often there is a middle person who is doing screenings or setting up initial interviews. They don't always work for that company so there's no direct contact there. The good thing about these apps is that they have the potential to be good for tracking the statistics on a job hunt. That is, *if* they're updated regularly. What I have seen happen more often than not is a minimal amount of back and forth and then nothing. NOTHING.

After a while, I find I have to go back to the app to see the job and then am not shocked to see it say "no longer active" or "job posting expired." What remains is a black hole with no explanation. Occasionally, it will say, "candidate was not selected," which actually feels a little bit better than nothing.

Still, I go back to wondering *why* I wasn't selected besides the fact that I didn't ever get a chance to talk to anyone.

The times I did hear back about a job were not all sunshine and rainbows either. Especially when I'd left the interview feeling excited and hopeful. While I appreciate having closure, I don't like a great interview ending in a letter telling me much they loved me but are not ultimately offering me a position.

Chapter 36:
We Know You Would Be Great, But....

I must be delusional. Really, there is no other explanation for the trauma I suffer after job interviews that went very well.

It seems like almost all my interviews go beyond simple question-and-answer sessions. We get personal, but not too personal. We banter about dogs, hobbies, family, or travel. I know they are secretly trying to find out more than they can legally ask, so I'm careful in my responses but share enough to titillate them into wanting to know more. Lately, I've tried to play the "my kids are grown and flown so now I have a lot more time and energy to commit to a job" card. I almost always leave an interview with the feeling that it went extremely well and that they will be calling again with a future interview or job offer. I just know it from the banter, the ease, the laughter. I know they will talk amongst themselves about how not only did I have the skills and experience for the job but dammit, how nice and funny and interesting I am as well.

Too often, I let my guard down about the job, saying to friends, "Based on my interview, I should have a job offer soon." I fall into my fantasy world again, the one where I get an actual paycheck, can pay my bills, buy new clothes, have a schedule, have colleagues and be successful, moving up through the hierarchy rapidly due to all of the aforementioned factors.

Cue the quiet. Crickets chirp. The sound of silence rushing through my ears. Day after day. After a few days I realize it's not going to be as I thought. I try to justify the reasons I have yet to hear back. Maybe they're contacting references, maybe someone important is away for a funeral. My ears, stretched as always toward any signs of contact, until, finally, a ping. The *Dear John* letter arrives.

"Dear Leslie,
We really liked you, but...."
"We know you would be great, but...."

But. But. But. BUT BUT BUT BUT...

But we have decided to go a different direction.
But we have hired someone from within the organization.
But your skills were not as strong as the person we ultimately went with.
But we have decided not to fill the position.
But we hope you will put your application in for future openings.
But we hope to see you at future networking events in our field.

What I read is:

But. But. But. BUT BUT BUT BUT...

But you are too old.
But you are a fraud.
But you won't fit in here.

But you are fat.
But you look like my ex-girlfriend.
But you are too talented and everyone else will be jealous of you.
But you should continue trying to get a job here for the next five years.
But what you have done career-wise so far is pathetic.
But you have wasted your life.
But you should have stayed on the farm.

How, then, does an employer let someone know that while they really enjoyed their time together, they never want to see them again? As the recipient of these messages, normally over email, but previously via regular mail, it causes me emotional pain, to dislike the organization and to doubt myself. I understand that in most cases there was a better candidate, and that we actually did have a positive exchange during my interview. That getting passed over for a job and having a fantastic interview are not mutually exclusive. There are times when I don't understand, of course, especially in cases where allusions were made to my onboarding, and my future office was shown to me in a tour wherein I was introduced to all of my future colleagues.

It once again feels like failing at dating apps. I could change a few of the words here and publish a dating book. Hmmm, hold that thought. In the meantime, let's talk about ways that this could feel better for the recipient of the bad news.

One of the oft-used methods to make a candidate feel better for the rejection is to tell them that a resume will be kept on file in case any further jobs come up. I would love to talk to even one person who has been contacted by a recruiter saying they had kept the resume for all this time and would you like to be interviewed for a position? I will eat my hat if this is common practice out there. I believe it should be, though, as what a savings in time and money for a company–just recruit from the resumes you already have! This is a known candidate and it will be a piece of cake. I would get a lot of calls, as well, from past interviews. To date,this number is exactly zero and I assume that's how it will stay.

"...***but*** *we went with someone who had a better combination of skills and experience.*" It's that sentence that really shoots an arrow through my heart. I know I'm capable of doing the work and in interview situations where I leave feeling like I have done a good job of answering questions as well as asking good ones, it always takes me by surprise. I feel like Charlie Brown kicking the football that is pulled away by Lucy, time and time again. I get that someone may do the job better at first. However, are they actually a better employee? I have the potential to be the absolute greatest employee that has ever been. I have proved my commitment to doing hard things, even mind-numbing things, as well as demonstrated my ability to be socially aware, ethical, compassionate, kind, and funny. Plus I bake bread! To hear NO chips away at my soul.

As a frequently-rejected applicant, I would love to feel validated as a human along with being seen as professional. In good interviews, ending with something as easy as "even if we don't end up working together, I'd like to connect on LinkedIn" would feel good. It validates the career side of things and is personal enough to feel good. Then, once the offer is off the table, a follow up note with a LinkedIn invitation will seem authentic. It's so much better than leaving a bitter taste in the mouth of the rejected applicant, never reaching out again and not acknowledging them for any of the work that they have done. I guess it boils down to simple advice I got from my grandma. "Always be considerate and kind."

Chapter 37:
BONUS CHAPTER for HR and Recruiters!

My editor told me that since this book is written for people like me, people who are trying to make a positive impact on the world and struggling to get traction, that no recruiter or HR professional would ever pick it up. To everyone who has found something useful in these pages, I am genuinely grateful. But I disagree with her, because I think every now and then someone who is responsible for hiring people stumbles onto exactly the book they did not know they needed. If that person is you, welcome. If you are in a hurry and came straight to this chapter looking for the good stuff, I respect your efficiency.

Before we go any further though, let me be clear about what this chapter is and is not. I am not a recruiter. I have never been a recruiter, and I have no inside knowledge of what it actually takes to manage a hiring process from the other side. There is a great deal I do not know, including the constraints, the internal politics, the impossible timelines, and the pressure that comes with filling a role that seventeen people have opinions about. Everything I know about recruiting I learned by being recruited, which is a little like learning to cook by eating at restaurants. I have strong opinions and limited expertise, and I own that completely. What follows are my honest thoughts about what I wish the process had looked like from where I was sitting, shared in the hope that it is useful rather than accusatory. If none of it applies to you, go ahead and read the whole book anyway. It is a good time.

Some rejections hit harder than others. Whether it was from a place I've wanted to work for a long time, an internal referral, a personal connection during the interview, finding out 19 school alumni also work at the same company, or somewhere I already work interviewing me for a promotion, some of the No's are not well-received. The most important thing, probably more important than just about anything to do with job hunting and interviewing, is the need for closure. Specifically, personalized closure. What this means is don't send someone a generic email that they did not get the job if there was an actual interview held.

In many instances, if there have been two, three, or four (or even more) interviews, the applicant is definitely envisioning their future at that company. Even if most of the interviews have been virtual, I can almost guarantee that the interviewee has searched out details about the employer, the workplace, and the coworkers, not in order to rule it out but to see how they will fit in. Often, later in an extensive interview process, the candidate has met many stakeholders, had a tour of "their" office space, talked logistics and onboarding and key dates and even benefits. When a rejection email comes through, usually after a painfully long quiet spell or mere hours after the last email (it goes both ways), it hurts pretty deeply–especially a generic message that says, "Thank you for applying; the position has been filled/is no longer available/has gone to a stronger candidate." In today's world, having multiple interviews leads the interviewee to believe they're wanted. The bomb drop of not even being addressed personally is a brutal ego blow, one that causes some of us (me) to hold lifelong grudges against certain organizations.

Sometimes, those secure in a position within an organization will interview for promotions. This causes a high level of both excitement and anxiety for that person, because it's even easier to envision the new job/office/coworkers since they are known entities. The anxiety comes from often not knowing who else is being interviewed and whether the potential for excellence has been appropriately noticed. *Has Tracy from accounting been talking about me behind my back?* Those types of things can cause ongoing stress and butterflies. The first solution is transparency by the interviewer, letting the candidate know what is happening as well as what the timeline is and who the competition is, if any. Share any past job reviews or documentation that the hiring team has access to and talk about anything that could be misconstrued. Don't take everything at face value, especially when the person you are talking to can discuss various situations. The worst thing that can happen is to open up the usual Monday email summary and see the lead sentence is "We are excited to welcome Jane 'Not-Me' Doe as our new Associate Director of the program that Leslie has been managing for the past ten years." Do not do this. Do not. Do. Not.

Many times, I have interviewed with people I know or have gotten a personal reference, which landed me in the hot seat for a job. This is a great way to network since the opportunity to be seen in person is rare and valuable. Nearly as many times, I have gotten a generic rejection letter. Way back in the olden days, I got a generic rejection letter for a job that I knew I was perfect for. Handwritten at the bottom, by one of the doctors I'd worked for, was, *"I really think you are so great and sorry this job didn't work out. Hopefully something better will come along soon."* That didn't stop the pain of rejection, but it did help cushion the blow. Please write a personal statement in the body of the letter. Be nice, be kind, be aware that the recipient is very human, even more fragile in that moment than most times in their life. Change, as well as anticipation of that change, is a big emotion. Don't kick them when they are down.

As mentioned earlier in the book, I have been trying to get a staff job at a local university for most of my professional life. I graduated from there in 1991 and worked there part-time for over a decade. I have gotten exactly *zero* in-person interviews from the dozens of applications that I have submitted. I am qualified and I know people. Somehow, I still get constant rejections, even when I use my insider information and name-drop. Maybe my skill set is not perfect for the job, but geez, please look at my experience with an open mind and see what I have done already. Maybe it's time to give me the chance to say my piece? For whatever reason, I have finally accepted that this particular employer and I are not meant to be.

Quick note here: if you see the same person's resume coming up for multiple jobs over a long period of time, it should be mandatory to talk to that person and see why they want to work there. It could be a game-changer for your organization.

Even jobs where I have had every single requirement have gone silent after submitting the application, followed by, "Sorry, we are hiring someone else that is absolutely, positively not you because you are awful and on the black list here, so stop applying for god's sake." Maybe it wasn't worded exactly like that, but there were a lot of generic rejections from personal connections that came across like that. Please do better.

You already know the process is broken because you built it, and you live inside it every day. Every candidate who has applied to one of your jobs has stared at their inbox like it personally owes them something, refreshed it at 2am, and quietly googled your company name plus the word "ghosting." More than likely, none of that comes as a surprise to you. So here is the thing, you do not need to overhaul the entire system to make a difference. You just need one email with one date and one sentence that tells a human being what to expect next, which you can write before your second cup of coffee. The candidate who receives it will not only feel valued as a human, they will also remember that you treated them like one.

While you are at it, do not overlook the people you already know. Run a mental list of former colleagues, past candidates, and anyone you worked with who impressed you enough to remember their name. Then actually reach out, with a real message. You may be surprised to find that the person you worked with three jobs ago is exactly what you are looking for right now, and they may be pleasantly surprised to hear from you. There is no shame in hiring someone twice, or in pulling a resume out of your files from two years ago and sending a note that says you have been thinking of them. (Remember, earlier in the book I claimed that this never happens, why not be the one that proves me wrong!) That is good recruiting. The best hire you ever make might be someone who already knows where the bathroom is.

Another big ask. Please don't let weeks or months go by while in the hiring phase. Each person who applies thinks they have what it takes to do that job. Do them a favor and treat them with some professional respect. Even saying, "we had so many candidates and think you would have been a good choice if you added a couple of certifications to your experience" will go a long way. If a job is on pause because Mary from accounting is on a long vacation, it would be great to drop a quick email to all of the applicants to let them know what the anticipated timeline is.

If you already have an internal candidate and you know in your heart they are probably getting the job, do everyone a favor and say so up front. External candidates are not naive, they fully understand that internal candidates often have a built-in advantage, and most of them can make peace with that. What they cannot make peace with is spending two weeks preparing for an interview, upgrading their wardrobe, driving across town, and performing their absolute best, only to receive an email three days later that says you hired someone from within. That email triggers an entirely unnecessary grief cycle that you could have prevented with one sentence during the screening call. If you are only considering external candidates who bring something your internal candidate doesn't, like an extra degree, a specific certification, ten more years of experience, please just say that. Most candidates will self-select and bow out gracefully, saving time, money, and dignity. The ones who stay in the running will know exactly what they are up against, which makes for a better interview anyway. Transparency is not a courtesy. It is just good recruiting.

Recruiting and hiring is hard right now! I know that, as do most people out there seeking employment. Let's be honest about the math. A single job posting can generate hundreds of applications, and by the time you have screened, shortlisted, and scheduled Zoom interviews, you are still looking at a dozen or more candidates for every open role. That is a lot of thank you emails landing in your inbox from people who are genuinely trying to do the right thing because every career coach on the internet told them to. So do them, and yourself, a favor and set the expectation before they even leave the virtual room. A simple "we appreciate the effort but please don't send follow up emails, we will reach out within two weeks (or by x/x/xx) with next steps" at the end of the interview costs you thirty seconds and saves everyone a lot of unnecessary inbox clutter and anxiety. You get to control the process, the candidate gets the closure they are desperately looking for, and nobody is left wondering whether their thank you note landed in spam. And if a handwritten note does show up in your actual physical mailbox, for the love of everything that is still good in this world, acknowledge it. That person went to a store, bought a stamp, and mailed you a letter in 2026. That deserves at least a nod.

Finding that sweet spot between overqualified and underqualified is genuinely hard, and most candidates understand that. They know their resume does not always land the way they intended, that a cover letter can undersell a perfectly good application, and that sometimes the fit just is not there no matter how much they wanted it to be. That part is fair. What is not fair is posting a job description that has been inflated (either historically, to justify a salary grade, or currently, to cast a wider net) and then interviewing candidates who showed up in good faith based on what you advertised. That is not a sourcing strategy. That is a bait and switch, and candidates notice. The ones who make it to the interview stage and discover the role is nothing like what was posted do not quietly accept it, they tell people. They write reviews. They remember. If your job description does not accurately reflect the role you are actually trying to fill, you are not going to find the right person for it no matter how many applications come through, because the right person opted out in the first paragraph. Accuracy in a job posting is crucial to have. It is the foundation of the entire process.

Let's talk about the application process for a moment, because candidates are not going to tell you this to your face. When you send someone to a platform that requires them to manually re-enter every single item from their resume into individual fields (looking at you GovernmentJobs.com) work history, education, certifications, references, each in their own little box, you are not screening for commitment. You are screening for patience, and those are not the same thing. A highly qualified candidate with options will abandon that application halfway through and apply somewhere else. The ones who finish are either desperate (ahem) or have nothing else going on (do you feel seen?), and neither of those is the filter you were looking for. You already asked for a resume. It is right there. It has everything you need, organized by a person who spent considerable time making it presentable. The redundant data entry marathon that follows is not a process, it is hazing. If your application platform requires candidates to spend an hour entering information that already exists in the document you just asked them to upload, it might be time to ask whether your system is working for you or against you.

I would be remiss not to acknowledge the elephant in the room, which is that artificial intelligence is rapidly changing the recruiting landscape in ways that would have seemed far-fetched even a few years ago. Resume screening, initial outreach, interview scheduling, candidate ranking-every day AI is doing more of this, and that is not going to slow down. But here is what AI cannot do. It cannot notice that someone's cover letter revealed a genuine passion for the mission of your organization. It cannot pick up on the energy of a person who is hungry and capable and just needs someone to take a chance on them. It cannot make a phone call to a former colleague and say "I think I have someone you should meet." The human parts of recruiting, the instinct, the relationships, the judgment calls, are still yours.

So that is my wish list. Thank you for indulging it, whether you are a recruiter who wandered into this chapter by accident or a job seeker who has been nodding along since page one. I am aware that some of this landed as a lecture and I make no apologies for that, but I do appreciate you staying until the end. If you are on the hiring side and even one thing in this chapter makes its way into your next process, then this book did its job. If you are on the job hunting side and felt seen somewhere in these pages, then this book also did its job. And if you are now wondering what kind of person sits down and writes an entire book about job hunting, I encourage you to go back to chapter one!

Epilogue

Chapter 38:
First Day Stories

You've come a long way, baby! We are getting close to the end of the book so I figured I'd drop a few fun stories in to reward you for your sticktoitiveness! After we accept a job, rework our wardrobe, buy a couple new pairs of shoes, and pack our lunch, it's time to head off to our first day like a kid starting kindergarten. You've likely been there, full of hope and excitement, not knowing what to expect. In many cases, it's pretty routine. First you show up at Human Resources, complete the hiring paperwork, get keys, a badge and an email address. Next, you're handed off to your boss, who shows you to your desk, introduces you to your coworkers, and tours you around the area. Maybe, on a good day, you are taken to lunch before being set loose to get your bearings. Sometimes, though, first days start off in ways that you will remember forever. These could be red flags or they could just be interesting stories. I want to share a few that were very memorable and that I will never forget.

Black Guy Pees

It was my first day doing community social work. Fresh out of college, I had hopes of doing good things and making a difference in my world. I was working with adults with a variety of developmental and/or physical disabilities who were living independently in the community, with the help from our agency. On my first day of work, I was taken out with a nice woman named Alexa. We visited a couple of her clients in their homes, helped with some routine tasks and then went to meet her next client at the grocery store. I'd been working as a personal care attendant for a few years for a young man who had cerebral palsy, so I was comfortable with the challenges of that particular disability. I knew we were meeting a client who had CP, who was ambulatory, hard to understand, and lived in an apartment nearby. We waited in the foyer of the grocery store. Suddenly, a young black man entered the store, somehow staying upright despite nature doing everything in its power to pull him to the ground. I still appreciate how hard it was for him to walk and how he didn't let his physical limitations restrict him. He grabbed a cart and we followed along while he added groceries from his list. Alexa was really good at understanding what he was saying. At one point, he said something to her while we wandered in the frozen aisle. She turned to an employee and asked him if her client could use the restroom. He directed him to go around the corner and into the back. Until recently, bathrooms in grocery stores were a rarity and you'd have to go use a random toilet somewhere in the back of the storeroom. We stood there as he rocked, zigzagged and swayed around the corner, heading through the storeroom doors. More time went on and we stood there waiting.

As more time passed, we started to worry that he needed help, but held our ground. One thing we didn't want to do is take away anyone's independence by stepping in prematurely or without being asked. So we waited. After a while we heard someone yelling what sounded like, "What do we do if the black guy pees?" We looked at each other with raised eyebrows, telegraphing the same thought. *Oh no, what if he went to the wrong area and had an accident?* The yelling happened again, "What do we do if the black guy pees?" We walked slowly to the end of the aisle and into the second freezer aisle. Standing with his head in a freezer, an employee was holding up a bag of frozen black eyed peas, yelling to a coworker, "What do we do with the black eyed peas?"

At that exact moment her client came back into the store from the back and wondered why we were laughing so hard. We could not explain, but our fears were erased and I learned a valuable lesson about making assumptions about people's capabilities, which is something I hold near and dear to my heart to this day.

The Grim Reaper

At another social work job, this time in a Skilled Nursing Facility, I was on a first day tour with one of my new coworkers. We saw the meeting rooms, the nurses stations, the break room and the various floors for different levels of patients. I would be working with patients in rehab who would be going back home after a short stay. Part of the building housed long term care patients. Sometimes they wandered around different floors and were gently redirected or escorted back to their rooms. On this first day, I was absorbing a ton of information, meeting a huge amount of staff, and trying to get my bearings. We were waiting by an elevator to go to another floor when the door opened and a small, elderly woman stepped out with her walker. She stopped, smiled at us, and fell to the ground, dead. Just like that. There was no warning. By this point in my life, I'd seen some things, but nobody had just fallen down dead in front of me at work. I stood quietly as the staff attended to the situation, quickly, gently and efficiently. Then the day went on as usual. It was pretty wild and, in that job, a definite harbinger of doom.

Rolling Out The Red Carpet

As a new employee, I was welcomed to my job as Operations Director at a fitness facility with balloons, flowers, a thorough and excited introduction to the entire staff, and given easy tasks which eventually became more complex, so that I was not overwhelmed. It was such a different welcome than I'd ever had, and I hope they know that I appreciated it so very much, despite my not staying there long enough. They were kind and supportive until (and even after) the end.

They also valued each of their employees, celebrating milestones, birthdays and taking the time to really get to know one another. I learned a lot from that job that I take with me as I interact with colleagues. It isn't hard to be kind!

Labor Pains

For many years, I collected costumes, wigs, accessories, makeup, shoes...you get the picture. It was a natural progression for me to work the Halloween season at costume shops. I started doing this way back in 1999, as a way to supplement my consulting income as well as to have a little fun and add to my collection. I got hired at a very big and famous Seattle costume shop. It was a great job, where every hour I could put on a different costume and all I had to do was go around and help people explore possibilities. It was awesome. However, my very first day on the job turned out to be a little crazy. Keep in mind that cellphones were not the norm yet.

I had just clocked in for my first shift and was walking around the store with the manager, meeting other staff and getting familiar with the lay of the land. Suddenly, a guy came up to me asking if my name was Leslie. *Um, yes.* He said I had a phone call, which was awkward, but I went to the desk and got on the line, with the manager looking at me quizzically the whole time, one eyebrow raised about this new employee and her use of the store's phone lines for her personal business. It was my sister-in-law calling. She and her husband shared the duplex with my partner and I. She was 9 months pregnant, home alone, and her water had broken. She wanted me to help her as her husband was at work and she couldn't reach him.

I explained to the manager that despite my first 15 minutes on the job being amazing, I was going to have to go and help with this baby situation. He was very understanding, and long story short, I got her to the hospital, found her husband, and the baby arrived with no complications. I got back to work the next day and resumed where we had left off. I spent a few Halloween seasons at that shop, and interestingly enough, worked many years at another costume shop (and still do), as it is one of my many hobbies that I ended up turning into work.

Doctor, Doctor!

I spent ten years (or more) with a side gig as a Standardized Patient. A standardized patient (SP) is a person trained to consistently and accurately portray a specific medical case, that allows medical students to practice clinical, physical and communication skills. Besides portraying cases (my "depression" was particularly good), I trained other students, hired students for a different program at a different medical school and even set up a national medical testing center, hiring and training dozens of SPs in the process. Not being a trained actor, I was still pretty good at my job. As an aside, I was often happy to find out certain students were going to be anesthesiologists, since their bedside manner was a bit lacking and it was best that their patients were unconscious. I digress.

I had a couple of kids along the way, as has been known to happen. We had lived in the city when the first one was born and were fortunate to have one of the best pediatricians around. He was kind, thoughtful, funny and pretty cute too. This will make more sense in a minute. A couple of years later we moved to the suburbs to continue to have kids. I sound like I had 14 kids but really, it's just two that I know of.

Where was I? Oh yeah, I got a Standardized Patient gig participating in some training for pediatricians, where they would have to talk to both a parent and the child about some different diagnoses. I was assigned a kid since mine were too young to be actors*. (*One is now a professional actor!) At the training, we got split into groups so we were with two pediatricians for our day. The doctors came into the fake exam room and we all stopped and stared at each other. It took a moment to realize what had just happened. It was really fun to discover that my first son's pediatrician was in my group. How random! And also our current pediatrician! The two doctors practiced their communication skills and we got to rate them before leaving for the day. (They both did well). Small world, though! It gave us a good laugh and I still question what the odds were of something like that happening.

Chapter 39:
Now What?

Now that we have gathered all the tools, gained the knowledge, learned the tech and gotten enough experience to get us a great job, we can ask ourselves, is it enough? How do we actually get our resume into the right hands and talk to the people who can get us the work we want? And the work–is it good work that fulfills us while doing good in the world? Is it even possible? For some of us, it's an ongoing battle to connect and prove our value. For others, the trajectory is a little less steep and jobs can be had. Most of us in our society must work, it's a given. Inheriting a few million dollars is nice, but there's only a few of those people out there. Most people get a little job in high school or college, attend college or get training and gradually work up the ladder in some way for the next 50+ years. The takeaway comes down to a few words! Be aware, be organized, be kind, be compassionate and be willing and able to meet others where they are.

Is this doable? Absolutely! Start slow and take little steps that make a big impact. Don't make yourself crazy! When looking for a job, take the time to get organized. Streamline your processes and check up on your online appearance. Do a scrub of everything you have posted out in the world. It may take a few days, but redo all your past employment information by aligning dates of hire and separation, and double check what you have entered for job descriptions in Indeed, LinkedIn to make sure they match your actual resume. Take a deep look at your resume and make sure it has the key words for jobs you want, and perhaps get another set of eyes to assess it and make any changes. Instead of 3,894,949 resumes, establish three or four main ones that you can easily edit for applications instead of always scrambling to recreate something new.

It is critical to touch base with your network. Beyond putting an "open for work" badge on your LinkedIn profile, it is crucial to maintain a list of former colleagues and employers. Reach out and tell them what you have been doing, what you want to be doing and see if they are in a situation to offer some insight on work or refer you to someone who is hiring. On top of that, prune your references list to your top champions and do a little caretaking of them. Meet them at their office, bring them a coffee, and have a discussion about jobs past and future. This assures that they will have a much easier time representing you during a reference check. It doesn't hurt to drop a few keywords that they can use to sum you up: dependable, enthusiastic, self-starter.....you know what you are capable of, make sure they do!

Don't forget to look before you leap. Do everything you can to research this opportunity. It is no fun to turn down a job offer when you need that money, but is saying yes to something that is inherently a bad match and could end up destroying years of your life worth it? Do you find yourself constantly applying for the same type of job and getting rejected? Perhaps obtain a new certification or get involved with a local group to gather more current information. Beyond all that, trust your instinct. I have ignored my red flags so often that I wonder if I'm color blind. What can you do to increase your awareness of the wrong situations?

If at all possible, don't justify taking a job for job's sake or because someone said you should, even if it feels wrong. Too often, it backfires and causes ongoing trauma and drama. Besides having to find a new position that is a better fit, you have to extricate yourself from a bad situation. Life is short, why be miserable?

Let me be honest with you. I do not have all the answers, but I definitely have more than I did in my twenties. You won't catch me walking the runway, that's for sure! What I can tell you is that somehow, while working on this book, I solved my own problem. The answer was in front of my face for years. It took writing an entire book about being 'Unemployable!' to see it. You really cannot make this stuff up.

Be aware	Of how the process feels on both sides. Your actions, your words, and your silence all land somewhere.
Be organized	A little structure goes a long way, whether you are applying or hiring. Know what you have, know what you need, and keep track of both.
Be kind	It costs nothing and it is remembered longer than you think.
Be compassionate	Everyone in this process is navigating something you cannot fully see. Give them the benefit of the doubt anyway.
Be connected	The next opportunity rarely comes from a job board. It comes from a person. Stay connected, follow up, and never underestimate the power of a genuine hello.
Be willing to laugh	This process is objectively absurd at times. A sense of humor will not get you the job but it will absolutely get you through the search.
Be where they are	Not everyone comes to the table the same way. The best outcomes happen when someone is flexible enough to close the gap.

Chapter 40:
Is this THE END?

Wherein I become a best-selling author and realize I have had the answer all along....

PUBLISH YOUR BOOK! The world has been shouting this at me for decades. Remember how I told you I started writing this book in 1998? It's about time that I let it out of my computer and put it into the hands of the world at large. I have high hopes, coupled with realistic expectations, of becoming a renowned writer. Many other books exist in my files, in various states of completion. With the final push, this one, my unpublished past becomes my whole new future.

My work may never be done. The many books I write may sell or they may not. Those are things I cannot truly control. I can control doing my best to finish them and get them out there in the world, and I can keep on working on making the world a better place in the meantime. I can speak to groups about a wide variety of experiences and outcomes and stories about my life in the trenches, which I do hope is a part of my future. And as always seems to happen, things shift again and there is more to add to the story.

I had decided, now that this book was done, to just work on writing and publishing. To heck with trying to be a grant writer! Of course, as is typical for me, I always keep my eye on the pulse of open jobs. *Indeed* popped an email into my box about a part-time grant writing position with a nonprofit that I really like, one where I'd even volunteered way back in the late 1980s! All I did was hit "click to apply" and it automatically sent them my resume. I didn't think about it again until they reached out to schedule an interview. Oh. Hmm. What's this? Long story short-I got the job and was kicking butt, writing some winning grants and enjoying the pace of my days. Then that opportunity ended, as suddenly as it appeared, leaving me once again wondering what I am supposed to be doing.

The book, Leslie! THE BOOK! Seriously, finish it and publish it, stop being so damn indecisive. So here we are. 'Unemployable!' is ready for its close up!

Postscript

Meanwhile, In My Inbox

The day I finally finished writing and editing this book, I felt like I had achieved something very significant. What I did not anticipate was that the universe, apparently unimpressed by my efforts, would continue sending me job opportunities at a steady pace. While I was busy polishing up my thirty years of job hunting, career pivots, and writing about the toll all of this takes, my inbox filled up yet again with some tantalizing new options for me! Here's an insight into my daily struggle to define who I am, and why the algorithms are both delusional and highly entertaining.

Chief of Staff, Microsoft

There are job postings that make you pause and consider the possibilities, and then there are job postings that make you wonder just what is going on at Microsoft. Chief of Staff at one of the largest and most complex technology companies on earth requires, at minimum, a working knowledge of technology. I have strong opinions about having to pay for an annual Microsoft Office subscription. I did not apply, though I appreciated the confidence. The one pro? It is walking distance from home!

Project Manager, Beavers Northwest

I do not know what Beavers Northwest does. Some things are better left as pure possibility. What I can tell you is that I spent several years on a Ragnar relay team called the Eager Beavers, and that we made a lot of beaver-related jokes over those years. When this posting arrived I felt, for one brief shining moment, that my entire life had been in preparation for something. For what? I still don't know. I remain available, Beavers Northwest, if you want to discuss the job.

Director of Security Operations, Microsoft

Microsoft appeared in my inbox again. Having reconsidered the Chief of Staff situation, they returned some months later with a revised assessment of my talents. Apparently since I am not suited to running their organization, I am ideally positioned to protect the entire company from cybersecurity threats for a salary exceeding $300,000 per year. I remain unclear on their reasoning. Again, I live pretty close so the commute would be great. And yes, I can definitely live on the salary. However, I can barely figure out how to turn my phone off and on, so I am probably not the strongest candidate here and will likely skip putting my name in for this one.

Head of Security, Seattle Symphony Orchestra

Around the same time Microsoft decided I had a future in security, the Seattle Symphony Orchestra arrived at a similar conclusion, albeit using my physical presence as a deterrent to all of those hoodlums who are out there threatening the string section. The Symphony is a beloved institution and I wish them nothing but the best. I also wish them a Head of Security who has some experience in security, which I do not. I do, however, have a very stern expression (OK, resting bitch face) that I have been told is quite effective in certain situations and I can squat over 400 pounds. Perhaps that is enough?

CEO, Classical KING FM

Having apparently canvassed the entire Seattle classical music security candidate pool, the universe pivoted once again to the executive suite. As Seattle's number one classical music station, this cultural institution, a beacon of civilization, decided that I am a good option for CEO. I am choosing to take this as a compliment rather than proof that the job search algorithm has completely lost the plot.

Co-Founder, Hyphen

Hyphen is a company. Or it will be, eventually, once it is founded, which it has not been yet. They are looking for a co-founder to help them become a company. I am a person who has spent thirty years trying to figure out what she wants to be when she grows up, and they are a company that has not yet figured out what it wants to be when it grows up. Apparently LinkedIn thought we should meet, and while I genuinely cannot argue with the logic, I am pretty sure my co-founding days are over.

Staffing and Recruitment Franchise Owner, Talentis Group

After thirty years of being on the receiving end of staffing and recruitment agencies, LinkedIn has arrived at what it apparently considers the obvious solution. I should become a staffing and recruitment franchisee myself. I should be the one making the hopeful calls and the promising leads and creating inexplicable silences. I should, in other words, become the thing I have spent thirty years navigating against upstream.

Development Manager, Model Railroad Museum of the American West

This one gave me pause for different reasons. My father spent his career with Burlington Northern Railroad. My oldest son was so obsessed with trains in his early years that he could identify locomotives by sight long before he could read. Trains have been a part of my family history in ways I never thought to examine until this posting arrived and something shifted unexpectedly. I sat with it longer than the others. I considered the commute and thought about my dad and my son. If it was The Thomas the Tank Engine Railroad Museum, I just might apply.

CEO, Tourette Association of America

"A perfect fit", said the subject line. After thirty years of job hunting, after every interview and rejection and gap year and pivot and moment of wondering why not me, the universe had been paying attention after all. It had waited, patiently, for exactly the right moment to deliver exactly the right opportunity. The Tourette Association of America needed a CEO. My first, immediate, unfiltered, completely involuntary reaction, the reaction I could not have stopped even if I had wanted to, was the most perfectly appropriate response I have ever had to a job posting in thirty years of looking. ██!

Field Staff Operations Manager, Polar—Lindblad Expeditions

Lindblad Expeditions would like someone to spend up to one hundred days a year traveling to some of the most remote and pristine locations on earth, driving Zodiacs, managing polar bear safety protocols, mentoring expedition leaders in Antarctica, and occasionally filling in as Expedition Leader on arctic voyages. They would also like this person to be certified in rifle operations for a polar bear habitat, which is honestly the most exciting job requirement I have ever read in my entire life. I am one hundred percent certain that this position was made for me. I am also one hundred percent certain that it was made for me in approximately 2002. I found this job at the very end of writing an entire book about finding the perfect career, which proves that the universe either has an extraordinary sense of humor or has been trying to tell me something for two decades and I was not paying attention. The ship has sailed, without me on it. Although, I wonder how hard it is to learn to drive a Zodiac?

The End

Acknowledgements

There are so many people to thank for the help in writing this book. First of all, my kids, Duncan and Spencer, for tolerating their mom's many career shifts throughout their lives. I could not do this without my sister, Barbie Applegate, for her undying support, hours of debate and a lifetime of laughter and joy, always my number one fan. To my partner, Russ Evenhuis, for his ongoing patience as I make him read, reread and listen to me read the manuscript so many times, not to mention his technical abilities that kept me from taking a sledgehammer to my laptop. All my love to Kristi Slotemaker, Bridget Horne, Suzanne Dawes, Anita Weinberg and Cat McDowell for reading the first version of this book and encouraging me to revise it without losing my voice. Shawn Lawlor gets a huge shoutout for not only being an early reader but for taking on my website design despite knowing in advance that I am technically challenged. Sierra Melcher and so many others in my group at Red Thread Publishing for the many years of Writer's Circle where I honed my voice and leaned into being comfortable calling myself a writer. Thanny Bradford for helping design my marketing materials, which are hopefully being worn around the world by now, shouting out this book's existence to the masses. I am so grateful to my advance readers for their feedback and comments, as I would not feel okay about putting this into the world without you. LaNorma Predmore, Leonard Damien, Carol Britton, Carol Evenhuis, Stephanie Aken, Caleb Powell and Diana Frank, thank you so much. Adrienne MacLaine, for her editing prowess and serious conversations about the final product. My life would not be the same without my first mentor, Elaine Schab-Bragg, who guided me along the way. Liz Rivelin for coming up with the subtitle for this book, which is exactly perfect. Jay Barber for creating my Elsie Press logo and imprint, along with thousands of hours of suffering through my career changes. So many of my former coworkers that experienced some of the wild and crazy jobs along with me. I hope you know how much I cherish the fact that we are still friends! Peter Brulla, Timothy Wolfe, Jennie Struijk, Sue Dowling, Stacey Buck, Jen O'Donnell, Holly Hinman, Crandall Chow, Ragna Sigrunardottir, Kyra Stewart, Rachel Crick, Lisa Latendresse, Lisa Cook-Craig, Jen Barber, Suzette Hart, Ann Humes, Greg Humes, Tamara Teague, all of my LUNA Chix teammates, and the PEPS moms that I will adore until the end of time, thank you from the bottom of my heart for being in my life. This book spans my entire adult life. As a result, I could go on and thank all of the drama kids, teachers and parents, the soccer families, my book clubs, my neighbors, dog families at the park and my bike friends, triathlon pals, volunteer groupies, college friends, and so on who have been a part of this adventure. I won't do that, instead I will send out this book into the world, ready for it to finally have come together in a succinct, entertaining and joyful way.

About the Author

Leslie Barber is a Pacific Northwest author, published poet, and comedy writer. She is the mom of two incredible young adults and two gigantic dogs. Her writing has appeared in Heart of Us: From Broken to Beautiful, Stories of Love and Life and FEISTY: Dangerously Amazing Women Using Their Voices & Making An Impact, winner of the 2024 Literacy Titan Book Award. UNEMPLOYABLE! is the first book from Elsie Press, and far from the last. Stay on top of future publications at elsiepress.com or https://elsiepress.substack.com/.

www.ingramcontent.com/pod-product-compliance
Lightning Source LLC
Chambersburg PA
CBHW031022160726
47991CB00005B/1838